comfort and joy

———————————— ≫·≪ ————————————

COMFORT and JOY

COOKING FOR TWO

Small Batch Meals for Every Occasion

CHRISTINA LANE

THE COUNTRYMAN PRESS · WOODSTOCK · VT.

The Countryman Press
Woodstock, Vermont
www.countrymanpress.com

A division of W. W. Norton & Company, Inc.,
500 Fifth Avenue, New York, NY 10110
www.wwnorton.com

For information about special discounts for
bulk purchases, please contact W. W. Norton
Special Sales at specialsales@wwnorton.com
or 800-233-4830

Printed in the United States of America

Library of Congress
Cataloging-in-Publication Data

Lane, Christina, 1984–
Comfort and joy : cooking for two /
Christina Lane.
      pages cm
Includes index.
ISBN 978-1-58157-342-8 (hardcover)
1. Cooking for two. I. Title.
TX652.L2459 2015
641.5'612—dc23
                              2015018975

10 9 8 7 6 5 4 3 2

—— »·« ——

To Camille.
I've loved you ever since the thought crossed my mind that you might be a sweet little girl growing in my belly.

To Brian. My rock. My love. My everything. This book would not have been possible without you. Every time a husband loads and empties the dishwasher for his pregnant wife, an angel gets its wings. There are so many angels in Heaven because of you.

—— »·« ——

CONTENTS

Introduction

First things first: I wrote this book while I was pregnant. Whew. It feels good to get that off my (rapidly expanding) chest. There were a few benefits to my "state." Mainly, food tasted absolutely amazing to me during my entire pregnancy. My mind flooded with cravings and flavor combinations all the live-long day. As I wrote and tested each recipe, I felt like an artist expressing myself in food. It was a good time to be a pregnant lady.

There were a few downsides, though. The larger my belly got, the closer it got to the flame. I bear a little scar on the right side of my belly from frying sausage for Angel Biscuits and Gravy one morning. I apologize immensely to my unborn child for this, but then again, I also hope to sometime tell her the story of how it came to be. I'm curious what will happen to the scar when my belly shrinks. This belly will shrink, right? Right?

The other downside was that the constant raucous in my brain of cravings made it hard to sleep most nights. I was kept up imagining the perfect ingredients for each recipe. I debated between Thanksgiving for Two side dishes for so long one night that I had to spray lavender oil in the room to calm myself down. And the perfect flavors for decadent weekend oatmeal? Oh, that led to an epic oatmeal-eating binge when I ate nothing but oatmeal for breakfast and lunch for weeks. Luckily, my doctor approved of my whole-grain and fresh fruit binge. I may have lied by omission about the crunchy sugar-crust topping, though . . .

Now that you hold this book, I'm probably snuggled in my perfect bed with my perfect baby that slept through the night, and my perfect husband has breakfast for two waiting for me on a perfect tray. KIDDING. Life is probably hectic with two dogs, a baby, and two jobs. The only hope I have for my future self is for weekend mornings. I hope that we can still manage to relax on Saturday and Sunday mornings and cook our favorite breakfasts from this book to enjoy in bed.

Although my weekday breakfasts usually consist of toast with an endless rotation of nut butters or smashed avocado, the weekends are when I pull out all the stops. It can be a chance for me to use up the veggies left in the crisper, or to make one of those extra-large breakfasts that holds us over until supper, giving us plenty of energy to accomplish yard work.

If I'm looking for something hearty to fuel us through a Saturday full of running errands or doing yard work, I always turn to big southern-style breakfasts. Where I'm from, grits are always savory, never sweet, and sometimes even spicy. I also proudly hail from the land of the breakfast taco, and you better believe this quick handheld, on-the-go breakfast has a permanent place in my kitchen. It just never gets old.

The lunch recipes that are included here are easy things that have been in rotation for years in my kitchen. From my first days of living on my own to the present — these are the things I commonly eat for lunch. I was so thrilled to finally put pen to paper and record these recipes. I've had friends stop by for lunch too many times, asking for my Smoky Black Bean Soup recipe or my Skillet Pizza recipe, only to have to shrug my shoulders and say, "I just winged it." Not anymore. Everything is written down here for you with precise measurements. Although the measurements are precise, please feel free to double or triple the recipes to feed your crowd. Savory recipes are easy to double, and I can certainly understand wanting leftovers of Green Chile Chili.

We have a habit in our house of treating Sundays the right way: with long and slow southern suppers. Both my husband and I, though we are Californians at heart, were raised in the South and grew up with leisurely Sunday meals. Not only is the food important on Sundays, but so is the way you eat it. I scaled down my southern favorites for you. I included some classics, too, because who doesn't love a pan of lasagne for a cozy dinner before another hectic week begins? The recipes of which I am the most proud in this section are my holiday meals. If you must spend the holidays without your family, at least you can have all the same foods without the leftovers. That said, we are known to make Thanksgiving for Two in the middle of the summer just for a taste of what's to come in November.

I'm sure you know, but petite desserts for two are my true passion in life. I included a small sampling of my favorites in this book. If you need more, just ask me. I'm always full of dessert for two recipes.

I hope y'all enjoy this book. I certainly had a fantastic time writing it.

Love and cupcakes,

Christina

⊱·BRUNCH·⊰

CLASSIC BUTTERMILK PANCAKES

I scaled down a recipe for a small batch of pancakes back in my college days. The minute the first few pancakes came out of the skillet, I wanted to eat. College girl was too hungry to wait for the rest of the batch to cook! This recipe makes six pancakes; that's two perfect stacks of three pancakes each. Plus, I promise the first pancakes will still be warm by the time you finish cooking the whole batch!

Yield • 2 stacks, 3 pancakes each

1 cup all-purpose flour

2 teaspoons baking powder

2 tablespoons granulated sugar

1 cup buttermilk

1 large egg, beaten

2 tablespoons unsalted butter, melted, plus more for griddle

½ teaspoon vanilla extract

Strawberry Coriander Compote (page 8), for serving

In a small bowl, whisk together the flour, baking powder, and sugar. Set aside.

In another small bowl, stir together the buttermilk, egg, the 2 tablespoons of melted butter, and the vanilla.

Meanwhile, melt extra butter on your griddle—the amount of butter really depends on the size of pan you're using to cook. If you're using a griddle with a temperature gauge, set it to 350°F.

Stir the wet ingredients into the dry ingredients. Stir until no dry pockets remain, but do not worry too much about lumps in your batter.

Using a ¼-cup measure, scoop out batter onto the preheated griddle or skillet. Cook until bubbles appear across the entire surface of the batter, and then flip to cook the second side until golden brown. Repeat with all remaining batter.

Serve with strawberry compote.

STRAWBERRY CORIANDER COMPOTE

I can be really bad about remembering to buy maple syrup for pancakes on the weekends, but fruit? I always have fruit. So, I tend to make a lot of fruit compotes for topping my weekend breakfasts. To this one, I stir in coriander, which may sound a little funny at first, but try it: it gives the compote a fresh, verdant taste.

Yield • 1 ½ cups

12 ounces strawberries (fresh or frozen are fine)

3 tablespoons agave nectar, honey, or sugar

¼ teaspoon ground coriander

Juice of ½ lemon

In a 2-quart saucepan, combine all the ingredients, except the lemon juice, over medium heat. Stirring occasionally, cook until the strawberries slump and slightly thicken, about 5 minutes.

Stir in the lemon juice, and taste—add additional sweetener if desired.

Serve with pancakes, waffles, yogurt, or oatmeal.

Store any leftovers in the fridge for up to 5 days.

LIGHT-AS-AIR, CRISP-AS-A-WAFER WAFFLES

To me, there is nothing more disappointing than a soggy waffle. Well, it's okay if *I* make it soggy with an excess of maple syrup or fruit compote, but fresh out of the griddle, it should be crisp and light as air. To make my waffle dreams come true, I add cornmeal to the batter for crispness. I also whisk the egg white separately — it's a little step that provides such a great reward.

Yield · 4 Belgian-style waffles

Neutral-flavored oil or cooking spray, for waffle iron

2 large eggs

½ cup milk

½ cup vegetable oil

½ teaspoon vanilla extract

⅓ cup fine-grind cornmeal

1 cup all-purpose flour

4 tablespoons cornstarch

2 tablespoons granulated sugar

½ teaspoon salt

½ teaspoon baking powder

¼ teaspoon baking soda

First, preheat your waffle iron to the highest setting. If it's not nonstick, have neutral-flavored oil or cooking spray ready.

Meanwhile, separate the eggs, and place the whites in a medium-size bowl, reserving the yolks in a separate bowl. Whisk the egg whites until stiff peaks form. You can do this by hand or using an electric mixer on medium speed. (It's important to whisk your egg whites first with clean beaters. Any trace of fat on your beaters will prevent them from properly whipping).

To the bowl with the egg yolks, add the milk, oil, and vanilla. Whisk to combine.

Combine the cornmeal, flour, cornstarch, sugar, salt, baking powder, and baking soda in a medium-size bowl. Whisk until very well blended. Add this mixture to the egg yolk mixture and stir until blended.

Fold the egg whites into the batter. Proper folding technique is down the middle with the skinniest part of the spatula, and then around the edges of the bowl. It will take a few minutes.

Once the egg whites are fully incorporated into the batter and the waffle iron is ready, grease the iron, and add ½ cup of batter. Close the lid and cook until done. My Belgian waffle iron requires ½ cup of batter per waffle, and this recipe makes 2 cups of batter, yielding four waffles.

Cook all of the batter, regreasing the waffle iron as necessary.

Serve with peach compote

PEACH-AMARETTO COMPOTE

Maybe a fruit compote with booze should be relegated to the weekends only. Just maybe. This is a judgment-free zone. Hey, Mondays are rough.

Yield • 1 ½ cups

1 pound sliced peaches (frozen is fine)

3 tablespoons agave nectar, honey, or sugar

1 to 2 tablespoons amaretto liqueur

In a 2-quart saucepan, combine all the ingredients, except the amaretto, over medium heat. Stirring occasionally, cook until the peaches slump and the mixture starts to thicken, about 5 minutes.

Just before serving, stir in the amaretto, starting with 1 tablespoon. Taste and add more if you like.

Serve with pancakes, waffles, yogurt, or oatmeal.

Store any leftovers in the fridge for up to 5 days.

PUMPKIN SPICE FRENCH TOAST WAFFLES

Whenever I can't decide between French toast and waffles, I make French toast . . . and cook it in the waffle iron! It's really a lazy girl's way of getting a waffle without a lot of effort. These "waffles" are a bit softer than traditional waffles, but since I like to use my waffles as a sponge for maple syrup anyway, it works for me! Another lazy tip: Substitute ½ teaspoon of pumpkin pie spice for all the spices in this recipe.

Yield • 4 waffles

¼ cup canned pure pumpkin puree

½ cup half-and-half

1 large egg

2 tablespoons light brown sugar

¼ teaspoon ground cinnamon

⅛ teaspoon ground ginger

⅛ teaspoon freshly grated nutmeg

Pinch of ground cloves

4 thick slices potato bread

Butter, for serving

Maple syrup, for serving

Preheat your waffle iron to the highest setting.

Combine the pumpkin, half-and-half, egg, brown sugar, and spices in a shallow dish. Whisk well to dissolve the pumpkin.

Once the waffle iron is ready, dip one slice of bread in the pumpkin mixture for 5 seconds. Flip and repeat. Transfer the bread to the waffle iron, and close the lid.

Cook until the waffle iron beeps.

Repeat with remaining three slices of bread.

Serve with butter and syrup.

QUICK (NO-YEAST) CINNAMON ROLLS

Easily one of the most popular recipes on my website, and for a good reason: Who doesn't love homemade cinnamon rolls in half the time? To avoid using yeast, these rolls have an almost biscuit-like preparation method. This gives them an ever-so-slightly different flavor than authentic yeast cinnamon rolls, but you'd be hard-pressed to get any complaints!

Yield • 4 cinnamon rolls

FOR THE ROLLS
Cooking spray or melted unsalted butter, for pan

¾ cup all-purpose flour, plus more for dusting

2 tablespoon granulated sugar, divided

½ teaspoon baking powder

¼ teaspoon baking soda

⅛ teaspoon salt

5 tablespoons milk

1 teaspoon cider vinegar

4 tablespoons unsalted butter, melted, divided

3 tablespoons light brown sugar

1 teaspoon ground cinnamon

Preheat the oven to 375°F, and spray four cups in a muffin pan with cooking spray (or use melted butter).

TO MAKE THE ROLLS: Combine the flour, 1 tablespoon of the granulated sugar, baking powder, baking soda, and salt in a medium-size bowl.

In a small measuring cup, combine the milk, vinegar, and 2 tablespoons of the melted butter.

Add the wet ingredients to the dry, and stir until a soft dough forms.

Heavily flour a work surface, and pat the dough out into a rectangle about 6 inches long. Use plenty of flour as you go.

Pour the remaining 2 tablespoons of melted butter on top of the dough.

Combine the brown sugar, cinnamon, and remaining 1 tablespoon of granulated sugar. Press this mixture lightly into the butter on top of the dough. Carefully roll up the dough, starting with a long side and rolling away from you. When you get to the end of the dough, pinch the entire seam shut.

Cut the dough into four equal pieces, and drop, cut side up, into the greased muffin cups.

Bake for 14 to 15 minutes.

FOR THE FROSTING

3 ounces cream cheese, softened

⅓ cup powdered sugar

Splash of milk or heavy whipping cream

TO MAKE THE FROSTING: Beat together the cream cheese and powdered sugar. If it seems hard to spread, splash in some milk or cream.

Frost the cinnamon rolls when they come out of the oven, and serve.

PECAN STICKY BUNS

The first time I successfully scaled down sticky buns for two, I made two buns. And I ate them both. Oops. So, now I make four buns and share them with my husband. I make my sticky buns in a jumbo muffin pan, but feel free to substitute a regular muffin pan or an 8-inch round baking dish. You will get a few more buns out of the recipe that way, and the baking time will be reduced, but everything will still be sticky and sweet!

Yield • 4 sticky buns

FOR THE DOUGH

½ cup warm water
(110°F)

1 ½ teaspoons active dry yeast

2 tablespoons granulated sugar,
plus a pinch for the yeast

2 tablespoons unsalted butter,
plus more for the bowl

1 ½ cups all-purpose flour,
plus more for rolling

MAKE THE DOUGH: Combine the warm water with the yeast and a pinch of granulated sugar. Stir gently, and let rest in a draft-free area for 5 to 10 minutes. At the end of 5 minutes, there should be bubbles and foam on the surface. If not, the yeast are dead; start over with fresh yeast.

Melt 2 tablespoons of the butter, and set aside to cool slightly.

Stir the remaining 2 tablespoons of granulated sugar into the foamy yeast, followed by the slightly cooled butter.

Place the flour in a medium-size bowl. Make a well in the center, and pour in the yeast mixture. Stir gently to bring the dough together, slowly adding flour from the sides of bowl as you go. The dough will be soft and somewhat shaggy.

Pick up the dough in one hand, and use your other hand to grease the bowl with the extra butter. Place the dough back in the bowl, flip to coat both sides with butter, and cover with a clean kitchen towel. Let rise in a warm area until doubled in size, 45 to 60 minutes. If your kitchen is cold, turn on the oven to 200°F for 5 minutes, turn the oven off, and place the bowl of dough inside.

FOR THE FILLING
6 tablespoons unsalted butter

½ cup chopped pecans

½ cup light brown sugar

¼ teaspoon salt

START THE FILLING: While the dough is rising, let the butter come to room temperature on the counter.

Once the dough has doubled in bulk, flour a counter and roll out the dough into a 10 × 6-inch rectangle. Flour the rolling pin and counter as needed as you work.

In a small bowl, combine the pecans, brown sugar, and salt. (Do not skip the salt; the buns taste flat without it). Place 1 tablespoon of this mixture in the bottom of each of four jumbo muffin cups.

Slice 2 tablespoons of the softened butter into four pieces, and place one piece on top of the pecan mixture in the bottom of each muffin cup.

Spread the remaining 4 tablespoons of softened butter over the rectangle of dough. Sprinkle the remaining pecan mixture on top. Roll up the dough into a tight log, and slice into four equal pieces. Place a bun, cut side up, in each muffin cup. Cover the muffin pan with a clean cloth, and let rise in a warm place for 30 minutes.

Meanwhile, preheat the oven to 375°F. Bake the buns for 20 minutes. Let the buns cool in the pan for a few minutes, to help the pecans stick to the buns instead of the pan. Invert the pan over a serving plate and let rest for a few minutes. The buns will fall out, and the caramel sauce will pour over the buns. Serve warm.

We spent the first leg of our honeymoon in New Orleans.
Our honeymoon, also known as "The Great Southern Road Trip,"
was when I got my first taste of true beignets at Café du Monde.
I made plans for us to visit several places for breakfast during our
stay, but needless to say, we went to Café du Monde every morning.
When I got home, I knew I had to perfect a small batch of those
golden, puffy delights.

A SMALL BATCH OF BEIGNETS

Yield • 8 beignets

2 tablespoons warm water
(110°F)

½ teaspoon active dry yeast

1 tablespoon granulated sugar,
plus a pinch for the yeast

2 teaspoons vegetable shortening

3 tablespoons milk

1 large egg white

3 tablespoons boiling water

1 ¼ cups all-purpose flour,
plus more for rolling

2 cups peanut oil

1 cup powdered sugar

MAKE THE DOUGH: Combine the warm water with the yeast and a pinch of granulated sugar. Stir gently, and let rest in a draft-free area for 5 to 10 minutes. At the end of 5 minutes, there should be bubbles and foam on the surface. If not, the yeast are dead; start over with fresh yeast.

Meanwhile, combine the tablespoon of granulated sugar, shortening, milk and egg white in a small cup. Whisk together well, then add the boiling water. Stir to combine, and then let the mixture cool slightly. Test the temperature of this mixture, and when it's between 105° and 110°F, add it to the foamy yeast mixture. Stir well. Finally, add the flour to the bowl, and stir gently to combine.

Cover the dough plastic wrap and let rest for 1 hour. You can make the dough ahead of time up to this point. I have kept dough for 3 days in the fridge before frying, and it was fine.

Heat the oil in a 2-quart pot to 360°F.

Meanwhile, divide the dough in half, and roll one portion into a 6-inch square on a floured countertop. Use a pizza wheel to cut into four squares.

When the oil is up to temperature, drop in the squares of dough. Fry for 1 to 2 minutes. When golden brown on the first side, flip the dough using a fork, and continue to fry. When that second side is golden brown (about 1 minute more), transfer the beignets to a cooling rack lined with paper towels.

Roll out the other half of the dough, cut into squares, and fry all the squares.

After letting them cool for about 5 minutes, dunk the beignets into the powdered sugar. Serve with all the extra powdered sugar piled on top.

RISE AND SHINE BLUEBERRY MUFFINS

Probably our favorite Sunday morning treat. I'm constantly finding muffin wrappers in my car because we usually eat them on our hurried way to church. Delicious muffins I can do, but being punctual for church, well, I'm still working on that one.

Yield • 6 muffins

4 tablespoons unsalted butter, melted

½ cup granulated sugar

1 large egg

¾ cup sour cream

1 tablespoon milk

½ teaspoon vanilla extract

½ teaspoon freshly grated lemon zest

1 cup all-purpose flour

1 ½ teaspoons baking powder

¼ teaspoon baking soda

½ cup fresh or frozen blueberries (if frozen, do not thaw)

Preheat the oven to 400°F, and line six cups of a muffin pan with paper liners.

In a medium-size bowl, stir together the melted butter, sugar, egg, sour cream, milk, vanilla, and lemon zest.

In a small bowl, whisk together the flour, baking powder, and baking soda. Add this to the wet ingredients, and stir gently to combine. Finally, stir in the blueberries.

Fill each prepared muffin cup with the batter— it will come almost to the top.

FOR THE STREUSEL

2 tablespoons granulated sugar

1 tablespoon all-purpose flour

1 tablespoon cold unsalted butter

TO MAKE THE STREUSEL: In the same bowl in which you mixed the dry ingredients, mix all the streusel ingredients together. Use your fingertips to work the butter into the flour and sugar. Sprinkle this mixture evenly over the six muffins.

Bake the muffins on the middle rack of the oven for 16 to 18 minutes, using a toothpick to test for doneness. Let the muffins cool for 1 minute in the pan, and then transfer to a wire rack to cool completely.

COFFEE CAKE MUFFINS

Because who doesn't want a little bite of cake for breakfast?

Yield • 4 muffins

FOR THE CRUMB TOPPING
¼ cup lightly packed
light brown sugar

1 tablespoon granulated sugar

Pinch of salt

¼ teaspoon ground cinnamon

1 tablespoon unsalted butter, melted

3 tablespoons all-purpose flour

FOR THE MUFFINS
¼ cup canola oil

⅓ cup granulated sugar

Pinch of salt

1 large egg

2 tablespoons heavy whipping
cream or sour cream

½ teaspoon vanilla extract

⅓ cup + 1 tablespoon all-purpose flour

⅛ teaspoon baking soda

⅛ teaspoon baking powder

¼ teaspoon ground cinnamon

⅛ teaspoon freshly grated nutmeg

Preheat the oven to 375°F, and line four cups in a muffin pan with muffin liners.

TO MAKE THE CRUMB TOPPING: In a small bowl, combine all the topping ingredients and use your fingers to pinch the ingredients together to make large clumps. Set aside.

TO MAKE THE MUFFINS: In a medium-size bowl, beat together the oil and granulated sugar with an electric mixer on medium speed for 4 minutes. Add the salt, egg, cream, and vanilla and beat for 15 seconds.

Sprinkle the remaining dry ingredients on top, and beat just to combine.

Scoop 1 ½ tablespoons of the batter into each prepared muffin cup. Top with a spoonful of crumb topping, and then divide the rest of the batter equally among all the muffin cups. Top the batter with the remaining crumb topping.

Bake for 19 to 23 minutes, until a toothpick inserted comes out cleanly and the crumb topping is golden brown.

BANANA BREAD BITES and CHAI WHIP

I can be a bit of a grouch in the morning,
especially when a recipe calls for softened butter.
Especially when I didn't remember to leave it out the
night before. Especially when the only butter I have is in
the freezer. I try to make all my breakfast recipes rely
on melted butter or cold butter, because I don't want
you to be grouchy in the morning. I want you to have a
mouthful of banana bread with chai whipped cream.

Makes 10 mini muffins

FOR THE BANANA BREAD BITES
Cooking spray

1 small overripe banana
(6 to 7 inches long)

3 tablespoons unsalted butter, melted

3 tablespoons granulated sugar

2 tablespoons honey

1 large egg yolk

½ cup all-purpose flour

¼ teaspoon baking soda

Pinch of salt

FOR THE CHAI WHIP
⅓ cup heavy whipping cream

¼ teaspoon ground cinnamon

⅛ teaspoon ground cardamom

⅛ teaspoon ground ginger

Pinch of ground cloves

2 tablespoons powdered sugar

TO MAKE THE BANANA BREAD BITES: Preheat the oven to 350°F, and spray ten mini muffin cups with cooking spray.

In a medium-size bowl, mash the banana very well with a fork. Stir in the melted butter, granulated sugar, honey, and egg yolk. Stir very well.

Sprinkle the flour, baking soda, and salt over the wet ingredients, and then stir to combine.

Divide the batter among the prepared muffin cups, and bake for 13 to 15 minutes. Test the muffins for doneness with a toothpick.

Let the muffins cool for a few minutes in the pan while you make the whipped cream.

TO MAKE THE CHAI WHIP: Beat together the cream with the spices and powdered sugar. Taste, and adjust the sweetness to your taste. You can make the whip a few hours in advance and store in the fridge, which sometimes I prefer because the spices dissolve better in the cream.

Remove the muffins from the pan, and top each with chai whip.

BRÛLÉED OATS WITH LEMON and MASCARPONE

Everyone knows oats and cinnamon go together, but I'm here to bring oats and lemon in style. Much in the same way that a simple bowl of oatmeal pops with a pinch of salt, lemon zest has the power to make a boring bowl of oats sing. Well, creamy mascarpone and a crunchy sugar crust doesn't hurt, either.

Yield • Makes 2 servings

1 cup rolled oats

1 ½ cups water

½ cup unsweetened applesauce

¼ teaspoon salt

1 to 2 tablespoons honey

3 tablespoons mascarpone

¾ teaspoon freshly grated lemon zest

Handful of toasted hazelnuts

3 tablespoons granulated sugar, for torching

Place the oats in a dry 2-quart saucepan, and toast over medium heat for 4 to 5 minutes while stirring constantly. Monitor their browning process (you can keep a few raw oats on the counter for reference, or let your nose guide you). Once the oats are toasty, pour in the water, applesauce, and salt. Bring to a simmer, and let cook gently until the oats have thickened, about 5 minutes over medium-low heat. Stir in the honey (as much as 2 tablespoons if you like your oats extra sweet).

Meanwhile, combine the mascarpone and lemon zest. Stir this mixture into the oats, along with the toasted nuts.

Divide the oats between two bowls, and sprinkle the sugar equally across both bowls. Use a culinary torch to brown the sugar until it's crispy. For an extra-thick sugar crust, torch the sugar in two layers — sprinkle half of the sugar on the bowls, torch it, let cool, and then sprinkle on the rest of the sugar and torch that.

Serve immediately.

EGGS BENEDICT

I'm a new devotee of eggs Benedict. I have been wrongly assuming all these years that hollandaise sauce tasted eggy, and why would anyone want to put egg sauce on eggs? Oh my gosh, was I ever wrong! Hollandaise tastes like sweet, golden butter. It is the nectar of the gods. I want to put hollandaise on everything now. I've even been known to dip French fries into it.

Yield • Makes 2 servings

2 English muffins

4 slices thick-cut bacon

¼ pound mustard greens or spinach

Salt, to taste

Freshly ground black pepper

4 large eggs

Slice the English muffins in half horizontally, and lightly toast them. Set aside.

In a medium-size skillet, cook the bacon until almost crisp. Remove it from the skillet, and let it cool and crisp on a plate. Leave the bacon grease in the pan.

Wash and chop the greens, and leave the water clinging to them before adding them to the pan with the bacon grease. Be careful of splattering oil.

Cook the greens until they wilt, about 5 minutes while stirring occasionally. Remove the greens from the pan and sprinkle with salt and pepper to taste.

POACH THE EGGS: In a 2-quart saucepan, bring 6 cups of water to a simmer. Once simmering, use a wooden spoon to swirl the water in one direction. You're trying to make a mini whirlpool. Once the water is spinning, slowly drop in one egg and poach for 4 to 5 minutes. The white should be cooked completely, but the yolk will remain soft. Repeat with other eggs. If you're an expert egg poacher, you can poach all of the eggs at once, and keep an eye on which eggs were first in the pot.

FOR THE HOLLANDAISE

1 egg yolk

1 teaspoon fresh lemon juice

Pinch of cayenne pepper (optional)

½ teaspoon salt

4 tablespoons unsalted butter, melted and kept hot

1 tablespoon hot water

TO MAKE THE HOLLANDAISE: In a blender, combine the egg yolk, lemon juice, cayenne, if using, and the salt. Turn on the blender to medium speed, and while it's running, very slowly stream in the hot melted butter. The sauce should emulsify. Leave it in the blender for now.

ASSEMBLE THE EGGS BENEDICT: Place the English muffin halves on each plate. Top each with a generous portion of greens, followed by a bacon strip cut in half. Gently add a poached egg on top of each piece of bacon.

Before serving, add the tablespoon of hot water to the hollandaise, and pulse one more time to blend. Pour the sauce over the eggs, and serve.

EGGS BAKED IN BAGUETTES (A.K.A. EGG BOATS)

Another excellent contender for a grab-and-go Saturday morning breakfast on the way to the hardware store. My husband and I both like to put our plant biology degrees to use a few times a year, and go crazy with landscaping our yard. A mini baguette stuffed with eggs and cheese can power us through planting shrubs, trees, flowers, and more!

Yield • 2 egg boats

2 mini baguettes

2 large eggs

⅓ cup cubed fresh mozzarella cheese

2 tablespoons fresh chives or basil

½ teaspoon salt

Handful of sun-dried tomatoes, chopped

Preheat the oven to 350°F.

Slice a V-shaped notch into the top of each mini baguette. Remove the bread from the inside of the baguette, but stop about ½ inch from the bottom of the bread. Dice the bread into cubes, and reserve ½ cup of cubes.

In a medium-size bowl, whisk together the eggs, cheese, chives, salt, and tomatoes. Stir in the reserved ½ cup of bread cubes.

Transfer the baguette to a mini baking sheet, and pour the egg mixture evenly into the baguettes. If the baguettes don't lay flat on the sheet pan, use pieces of foil to prop them up. Carefully place in the oven, and bake for 23 to 25 minutes. Poke the egg mixture in a few places with a toothpick to make sure the eggs aren't runny. Serve immediately.

It was really hard for me to decide if six biscuits would
serve two people. I thought it was too many at first. Then,
I made them, and two people cleared six biscuits one morning
before eight a.m. I guess we cleared that up real quick!

You'll notice this biscuit recipe uses mostly shortening.
Within this book, you'll also find a biscuit recipe that uses
half-butter, half-shortening, and one that uses neither.
I like to give you lots of biscuit options, because
I've never met a biscuit I didn't like.

A HALF-DOZEN BUTTERMILK BISCUITS

Yield • 6 biscuits

1 ⅓ cups all-purpose flour, plus more for dusting

½ teaspoon salt

1 ¼ teaspoons baking soda

½ teaspoon baking powder

2 tablespoons shortening, cold

1 ½ tablespoons cold unsalted butter, plus more, melted, if desired

½ cup buttermilk, plus more if needed

Preheat the oven to 450°F and have ready a 6-inch round pan or a 6-inch cast-iron skillet.

In a small bowl, whisk together the flour, salt, baking soda, and baking powder.

Cut the shortening and the 1 ½ tablespoons of butter into small pieces and add it to the flour mixture, cutting it in with a pastry cutter or two knives. When all the pieces of fat are the size of rice grains and are evenly coated in flour, pour in the buttermilk. Knead the dough lightly, and add additional buttermilk, 1 tablespoon at a time, if the dough seems dry or crumbly.

Tip the dough out onto a floured counter and pat it out to 1 inch thick. Dip a 3-inch biscuit or cookie cutter in flour and cut out four biscuits. Gather up the scraps and gently pat them out in order to cut out two more biscuits.

Arrange the biscuits in the ungreased pan—you want the biscuits to be closer together. Bake for 10 minutes, or until lightly golden on top. If you want, brush with extra melted butter as they come out of the oven.

BACON PARMESAN BISCUITS

A little riff on my standard buttermilk biscuits.

Yield • 4 biscuits

1 ⅓ cups all-purpose flour

½ teaspoon salt

1 ¼ teaspoons baking soda

¾ teaspoon baking powder

½ cup grated Parmesan cheese

2 tablespoons vegetable shortening, cold and diced

2 tablespoons unsalted butter, cold, divided

½ cup buttermilk

2 slices baked bacon, chopped (see page 58)

Preheat the oven to 450°F.

In a medium-size bowl, stir together the flour, salt, baking soda, baking powder, and Parmesan.

Add the shortening and 1 ½ tablespoons of the butter, and work it through the dough, using your fingertips or a pastry cutter. The butter should be evenly dispersed and smaller than peas.

Stir in the buttermilk and chopped bacon. Stir a few times to bring the dough together, then pour the dough onto a well-floured counter.

Bring the dough together into a ball, then press out into a 5 × 5-inch square about 1 inch thick. Using a knife, cut the dough down the middle both ways, into four equal squares.

Melt the remaining ½ tablespoon of butter, and brush it over each biscuit.

Transfer the biscuits to a small, ungreased sheet pan, and bake for 10 minutes. Let cool on the pan for 1 minute, then serve immediately.

ANGEL BISCUITS AND GRAVY

Admittedly, I'm a sweets-for-breakfast type of gal these days. It kinda goes along with my "Queen of Desserts for Two" territory. But my husband raved about his stepmom's biscuits and gravy for so long that I finally had to try my hand at them. I knew I wanted to scale down my standby recipe for angel biscuits. Angel biscuits are great because they come together quickly with just flour, cream, and one leavener. Once I realized that sausage gravy was easy to whip up in one pan, I started making this dish regularly.

Yield • 4 small biscuits with gravy; serves 2

FOR THE GRAVY
½ pound ground sausage meat (spicy or sweet, your choice)

2 tablespoons all-purpose flour

½ cup heavy whipping cream

1 cup milk

FOR THE BISCUITS
1 cup all-purpose flour, plus more for rolling

1 ½ teaspoon baking powder

½ teaspoon salt

¾ cup heavy whipping cream, plus more for brushing

Preheat the oven to 400°F.

TO MAKE THE GRAVY: Place the sausage meat in a small skillet over medium-high heat. Brown the meat, using a wooden spoon to break it into pieces as it cooks. When the meat no longer has any pink color to it, lower the heat to medium-low, and sprinkle with the flour. Let cook for 1 to 2 minutes while constantly stirring. Stir in the cream and milk. Bring to a simmer and cook for 3 to 5 minutes, or until the mixture thickens and coats the back of a spoon.

TO MAKE THE BISCUITS: In a medium-size bowl, whisk together the flour, baking powder, and salt. Make a well in the middle, and pour in all the cream at once. Stir gently until a shaggy dough forms. You may need to add a splash more cream to moisten the flour at the bottom of the bowl.

Turn out the dough onto a floured surface, and pat the dough into a 5-inch circle. Using a small biscuit cutter, cut out four biscuits.

Transfer the biscuits to a nonstick baking sheet or small cast-iron skillet, and brush with an extra layer of cream.

Bake for 10 to 14 minutes, or until golden brown on top,

Divide the gravy between two plates, and serve two biscuits on top of each serving of gravy.

CROISSANTS

I've long wanted to spend my Sunday mornings eating a croissant and sipping strong coffee like a French woman. There are a few issues with that picture for me, though: one, I prefer tea, and two, all baked goods in my house are homemade. When I started looking at homemade croissant recipes, I realized that most recipes make enough croissants for a large crowd. So, my scale-it-down attitude came into play, and I scaled it down to make four beautiful croissants.

And also like a French woman, I wanted the baking process to be effortless. So, I took a cue from Mireille Guiliano and divided the process into easy steps over three days. This way, I start on Friday and end up with croissants Sunday morning, just as planned.

Don't be intimidated by this recipe — the worst that can happen is that your hands fumble the dough and the folding process gets a little haphazard. Still, you'll end up with homemade crescent rolls, which aren't too bad, either.

Yield • 4 croissants

½ cup + 1 tablespoon 2% milk, divided

2 teaspoons active dry yeast

1 cup + 2 tablespoons all-purpose flour, divided, plus more for rolling

1 tablespoon granulated sugar

¼ teaspoon salt

6 tablespoons high-quality butter (high-fat European-style is great)

1 large egg yolk, beaten

DAY ONE: Heat ½ cup of the milk to 115°F, and stir in the yeast until dissolved. Stir in 1 tablespoon of the flour. Let sit until foamy, about 5 minutes.

In a medium-size bowl, mix the sugar, remaining 1 cup + 1 tablespoon of the flour, and salt. Add the foamy yeast to the mixture, and knead until smooth with a wooden spoon, 3 to 4 minutes. The dough will be sticky, but it will stick to itself and not the edges of the bowl. Refrigerate overnight.

DAY TWO: Let the butter come to room temperature.

Remove the dough from the fridge (it should have risen some and seem bubbly). Flour a surface, and roll out the dough into a 6 × 10-inch rectangle; the 6-inch side should be closest to you.

Spread 6 tablespoons of the butter evenly over the rectangle, but leave about 1 cm of a border on all edges.

FOLD THE DOUGH LIKE A LETTER: fold the top third toward the middle, then fold the bottom third upward, to layer over the top third. Again roll out the dough into a 6 × 10-inch rectangle. Cover and refrigerate the dough rectangle for 2 hours.

Remove the dough from the fridge after 2 hours, fold it like a letter again, and then roll back out to a 6 × 10-inch rectangle. Place it back in the fridge for 2 hours.

Repeat this two more times for a total of four folds, refrigerating for 2 hours between each fold and roll. After the last roll-out, refrigerate the dough overnight.

DAY THREE Remove the dough from the fridge, and roll it out into a 10-inch square on a floured surface.

Using a knife, cut the square diagonally both ways into four equal-size triangles. Roll up the triangles, starting at the wide end and rolling toward the skinny tip.

Place the rolls on a baking sheet lined with a nonstick mat, and brush with the remaining tablespoon of milk.

Let the rolls rise until doubled in size, about 1 hour. If your kitchen is cold, let them rise for longer—they really need to double in size before baking.

Preheat the oven to 400°F. Brush the egg yolk generously over the croissants. Be sure to get it in the nooks and crannies of the dough.

Bake for 10 to 15 minutes, until very golden brown. Start checking on the rolls at 10 minutes, and shield them with foil if the edges threaten to burn. You just spent 3 days making rolls, so keep an eye on them in the oven so they don't burn!

Let cool for 20 minutes on the baking sheet and serve.

CHOCOLATE CROISSANTS, NATURALLY

Naturally, if you make my small batch of croissants, it will cross your mind to stuff the dough will all sorts of delicious things when rolling them up. Can I recommend chocolate chunks? Actually, can I *highly* recommend chocolate chunks? You won't regret it. An extra brushing of butter and a sprinkling of cinnamon sugar is nice, too.

Yield • 4 croissants

1 recipe Croissants (page 44, reserving the last tablespoon of milk and the egg for brushing)

All-purpose flour, for rolling

⅓ cup chopped chocolate

Follow the instructions for the small batch of croissants on page 44 all the way through Day 2.

On Day 3, remove the dough from the fridge, and roll it out into a 6 × 12-inch rectangle on a floured surface.

Using a knife, cut the rectangle into four smaller rectangles of equal size.

On one side of each rectangle, place a heaping tablespoon of chocolate chunks.

Starting on a short edge of each rectangle, roll the dough into a cylinder.

Place the rolls on a baking sheet lined with a nonstick mat or parchment paper, and brush with the remaining tablespoon of milk.

Let the rolls rise until doubled in size, about 1 hour. If your kitchen is cold, let them rise for longer— they really need to double in size before baking.

Preheat the oven to 400°F.

Brush the egg yolk generously over the croissants. Be sure to get it in the nooks and crannies of the dough.

Bake for 10 minutes. Check on the rolls, and shield them with foil if the edges threaten to burn. Bake for another 2 minutes if the rolls aren't very golden brown.

Let cool for 20 minutes on the baking sheet, and then serve.

FLAKY SAUSAGE POCKETS

I spent the better part of fall one year perfecting an easy recipe for puff pastry. I never seem to remember to buy it at the store — probably because I forbid myself from walking down the frozen foods aisle, lest sixty pints of ice cream find their way into my grocery cart. Puff pastry is such a versatile ingredient to have on hand, however. This recipe for fifteen-minute puff pastry saves the day. It comes together in, you guessed it, fifteen minutes, and can be used for savory or sweet recipes. Here, I stuffed the dough with sausage, cream cheese, and scallions for a quick grab-and-go breakfast.

Yield • 6 pockets

FOR THE 15-MINUTE PUFF PASTRY
1 cup (125 grams) all-purpose flour,
plus more for dusting

¼ teaspoon salt

10 tablespoons cold unsalted butter

¼ to ⅓ cup cold water

TO MAKE THE 15-MINUTE PUFF PASTRY: Combine the flour and salt in a medium-size bowl.

Dice the butter, and add it to the flour. Using your fingers or a pastry cutter, work the butter into the dough until it's evenly distributed and roughly the size of peas.

Make a well in the center of the dough, and pour in the water, starting with ¼ cup first. If the dough seems dry, add an additional tablespoon of water.

Stir until the dough comes together, then place it on a well-floured surface. Roll the dough away from you into a 10-inch rectangle. Fold the dough into thirds like a letter: fold the bottom third of the dough toward the middle and cover that with the top third of the dough. Rotate the dough 90 degrees, and roll the dough back into a 10-inch rectangle, fold like a letter, and rotate 90 degrees. Repeat this process four or five more times, for a total of six or seven rolls. This creates the flaky butter layers in the dough.

It's entirely optional, but I recommend letting the dough rest, covered, in the fridge for 1 hour before use. You can do this up to 2 days in advance.

2 sausage links
(a little less than a ½ pound total)

3 ounces cream cheese, softened

2 scallions, sliced

Freshly ground black pepper

1 large egg yolk

TO MAKE THE FILLING: Remove the sausage from the casings and brown the meat in a small skillet. Use a wooden spoon to break up the lumps as much as possible. Drain the sausage meat.

In a small bowl, stir the sausage meat together with the cream cheese, scallions, and pepper. Taste and adjust seasoning—you may want to add additional salt. Chill the mixture in the fridge during the next steps (or does this up to 1 day in advance and chill overnight).

Preheat the oven to 400°F, and line a baking sheet lined with parchment paper.

Roll out the dough into a 12 × 16-inch rectangle. Using a dough cutter, cut three vertical lines in the dough, each 4 inches apart. Next, cut four horizontal lines in the dough, each 4 inches apart, for a total of twelve squares of dough.

Divide the sausage mixture into six equal piles, and scoop one onto each dough square. Gently press the sausage mixture flat, leaving a ½-inch margin around all the edges.

Press one of the six remaining dough squares on top of each mound, and use your fingers to gently seal the edges together. Use the tines of a fork to crimp the edges sealed.

Brush the egg yolk evenly over the dough, covering all edges.

Bake for 20 minutes on the baking sheet, until golden brown and puffy.

≫· APPLE TURNOVERS

Another way to use my easy 15-Minute Puff Pastry dough, but this time, with sweet apples and cinnamon!

Yield • 4 turnovers

2 cups peeled, cored, and diced apple (about 3 small apples)

1 teaspoon ground cinnamon

1 tablespoon fresh lemon juice

¼ cup light brown sugar

1 tablespoon unsalted butter

Pinch of salt

1 recipe 15-Minute Puff Pastry (page 51)

1 large egg yolk, beaten

Coarse sugar, for sprinkling on top (optional)

Preheat the oven to 400°F, and line a large baking sheet with parchment paper.

In a small skillet over medium-low heat, place the diced apple, cinnamon, lemon juice, brown sugar, butter, and salt. Cook, stirring occasionally, until the apple softens and caramelizes, about 7 minutes.

Remove the apple mixture from the skillet and let cool while you work with the dough.

Roll out the dough into a 12-inch square on a floured surface. Use plenty of flour as you go, to prevent sticking.

Divide the apple mixture into four equal piles in the four corners of the dough, making sure to leave a ¾-inch border from the edges of the dough. Cut the dough into four equal squares, then fold over diagonally to make four triangles. Crimp the edges closed with the tines of a fork.

Carefully move the pies to the baking sheet, and brush with the beaten egg yolk. Sprinkle with coarse sugar, if using.

Bake for 20 minutes, until the pies are puffy and very golden brown. Serve warm.

SHORTCUT BREAKFAST POTATOES

I'm not one to shy away from cooking a three-course dinner party, but perfect breakfast potatoes with a crispy crust and fluffy interior? They gave me nightmares. Sometimes, the only reason I would be willing to go out for brunch is to get a perfectly cooked potato. For years, when I'd try to make them myself, I would burn the outside before the inside cooked. I would add more and more oil to the pain to compensate. I would constantly adjust the heat. Enough, I said! And I bought frozen ones. But now, I've figured it out. And I couldn't be happier with the results! I cook the potatoes in the microwave before I fry them on the stove. Not only does this save me time, but it gives me perfectly crisp breakfast potatoes every time. You'll think you're at brunch!

Yield • Makes 2 servings

1 pound russet baking potatoes

2 tablespoons neutral-flavored oil

1 tablespoon unsalted butter

1 teaspoon grill seasoning

Wash the potatoes, prick them with a fork, and wrap each in its own paper towel.

Microwave on high for 3 to 5 minutes, or until the potatoes are mostly done in the middle. A little firmness is okay.

Carefully remove the potatoes from the microwave and dice them into bite-size pieces. They will be hot!

Meanwhile, heat the oil and butter in a nonstick skillet over medium heat. Add the diced potatoes, stir once, and let them cook undisturbed for a few minutes. Once a golden brown crust appears on one side, stir, and continue to cook until all sides are golden brown. Just before removing them from the pan, stir in the grill seasoning. Serve immediately.

≫· BAKED BACON
(the only way to cook bacon, ever)

Let me count the ways I love baked bacon. One, it frees up your hands to scramble eggs. Two, no more splattering mess on my stovetop. Three, the bacon stays flat instead of twisting and turning in the pan. Four, I love bacon because bacon is bacon. Or is it because bacon is bakin'?

I take it a step further and slide the pan into the oven while it's pre-heating. In my mind, this makes it finish cooking faster, but I could just be tricking myself.

4 slices bacon (or as many as fit on a pan not touching)

Line a sheet pan with ½ inch sides with foil.

Arrange the bacon slices flat on the pan, not touching.

Slide the pan into the oven, and set the heat at 375°F. Cook for 10 minutes, flip, and cook for another 10 minutes, until the bacon reaches desired level of crispness. The bacon will crisp when it cools, so I pull the bacon out when it feels firm, and little bubbles are all over the surface.

Blot the bacon lightly before serving. So meaty!

SWEET POTATO PIE GRANOLA

This is your weekend granola. Your slightly decadent, maybe-too-much-butter-but-hey-it's-the-weekend granola.

Yield • 4 cups granola

1 small sweet potato (about 4 ounces)

6 tablespoons unsalted butter

½ cup light brown sugar

½ teaspoon vanilla extract

2 cups rolled oats

½ teaspoon ground cinnamon

½ teaspoon freshly grated nutmeg

¼ teaspoon ground allspice

¼ teaspoon salt

⅓ cup pecan halves

Preheat the oven to 350°F. Grease a sheet pan.

Wrap the sweet potato in a paper towel, and microwave on high until tender, 3 to 5 minutes. Let cool, then peel.

Meanwhile, melt the butter in a small skillet over medium-low heat, and let it brown. The white foam in the butter will become brown, and the crackling sound will stop. Keep a close eye on it so it doesn't burn. Remove it from the heat and let cool slightly.

Add the peeled sweet potato to the butter mixture, and mash together very well with a fork. Stir in the brown sugar and vanilla.

In a medium-size bowl, combine the oats, spices, salt, and pecans. Add the sweet potato mixture to the bowl, and stir to evenly distribute everything.

Spread the mixture on a prepared sheet pan, and bake for 10 minutes.

Stir, and bake for another 10 to 15 minutes, until golden brown and crisp. Let cool, and serve. Store any leftovers in an airtight container for up to 1 week.

OVERNIGHT ICED COFFEE

I'm so glad that iced coffee became such a trend, because it is truly delicious. I always wondered how the coffeehouses got such a dark, robust flavor. I wrongly assumed iced coffee was just chilled leftover coffee. Now, I know the ways of iced coffee making from a friend who worked at one of those fancy coffee shops. And now you do, too! Don't be afraid of the citrus juice — you won't taste it, but the extra acidity makes the flavor of the beans shine through.

Yield • 2 servings

FOR THE COFFEE
2 cups cold filtered water

¼ cup finely ground dark-roast beans

1 tablespoon fresh lemon or orange juice

Coconut milk or cream, for serving

FOR THE COCONUT SYRUP
½ cup coconut water

½ cup coconut sugar or granulated sugar

TO MAKE THE COFFEE: In a large French press (or regular bowl), stir together the cold water, coffee beans, and juice. Cover, and place in the fridge overnight, or for at least 8 hours.

TO MAKE THE COCONUT SYRUP: Combine the coconut water and coconut sugar in a small saucepan, and heat over medium heat, stirring, until the sugar fully dissolves. Let cool, and chill in the fridge overnight.

In the morning, press the French press down (or strain the mixture out of the bowl). Divide between two cups, add as much coconut syrup as you like, and top with coconut milk to taste.

Store any leftover coconut syrup covered in the fridge for up to 2 weeks.

CHAI LATTES

If there's one thing that keeps me going to coffee shops, it's chai lattes. I can be hit or miss on drinking coffee, but a chai latte always sounds good. I started making them at home a few years ago when I lived too far away from a coffee shop. I usually double this recipe and get a few days' worth of lattes out of it — hold off on the milk until just before serving, though.

Yield • 2 lattes

2 cups water

1 (2-inch) piece of fresh ginger, peeled and thinly sliced into coins

1 cinnamon stick, broken in half

3 cardamom pods, crushed

3 whole cloves

2 whole black peppercorns

1 whole star anise

2 black tea bags

½ teaspoon vanilla extract

2 tablespoons honey, plus more to taste

Milk or cream, for serving

In a small saucepan, combine the water, ginger coins, cinnamon stick, cardamom pods, cloves, peppercorns, and star anise. Bring the mixture to a simmer, lower the heat, cover, and simmer for 10 minutes. After 10 minutes, turn the heat off and add the tea bags. Cover and let steep for 10 minutes.

Strain the mixture to remove the spices and tea, and then stir in the vanilla and honey. Taste for sweetness, and add more honey, if desired.

To serve, divide the mixture between two mugs, and top with as much milk or cream as you like. To be even more authentic, froth the milk in a milk frother, or heat on the stove and whisk until frothy before pouring over the tea.

⟫⟫· PUMPKIN SPICE LATTES

I'll just go ahead and admit it: I drink these almost year-round. I don't even wait for the major coffee shops to start making them in the fall; the minute the first leaf changes, I pull out my can of pumpkin.
I'm almost positive none of the coffee shop versions have real pumpkin in them, so consider this an upgrade! This is the basic version, but see page 69 for a chocolate version!

Yield • Makes 2 servings

½ teaspoon pumpkin pie spice
(see homemade recipe)

2 tablespoons canned pure
pumpkin puree

2 tablespoons honey

1 ½ cups milk

2 tablespoons vanilla extract

2 shots espresso or ⅔ cup strong coffee

Whipped cream, for serving

In a small saucepan over medium heat, combine the spices, pumpkin, and honey. Cook, stirring constantly, until it starts to simmer, about 45 seconds.

Stir in the milk and vanilla. Bring to a slight simmer while constantly stirring.

Using an immersion blender (or carefully transfer the mixture to a blender), blend until frothy.

Divide the espresso between two glasses, and divide the latte mixture on top. Top with whipped cream and serve.

Homemade Pumpkin Pie Spice

(makes 2 tablespoons)

1 tablespoon ground cinnamon

2 teaspoons ground ginger

½ teaspoon ground cloves

½ teaspoon ground allspice

1 teaspoon freshly grated nutmeg

½ teaspoon freshly ground
black pepper

Combine all the ingredients, and store in an airtight container.

PUMPKIN MOCHAS

In case you need a little chocolate to get your mornings going . . .

Yield • Makes 2 servings

½ teaspoon pumpkin pie spice
(see page 66 for homemade recipe)

2 tablespoons canned pure
pumpkin puree

2 tablespoons honey

1 ½ cups milk

2 tablespoons vanilla extract

¼ cup store-bought chocolate sauce,
plus more for garnish

2 shots espresso or ⅔ cup strong coffee

Whipped cream, for serving

In a small saucepan over medium heat, combine the spice blend, pumpkin, and honey. Cook, stirring constantly, until it starts to simmer, about 45 seconds.

Stir in the milk and vanilla. Bring to a slight simmer while stirring constantly.

Using an immersion blender (or transfer the mixture carefully to a standing blender), blend until frothy.

Pour 2 tablespoons of chocolate sauce into each glass. Divide the espresso equally between the glasses. Pour the frothy pumpkin latte mixture on top, then top with whipped cream. Drizzle extra chocolate sauce on the whipped cream.

DIY "TEA" BLENDS

I'm a hot tea kind of a gal at heart. Even during the summer, I need to start my days with something warm to sip on, and tea is often my choice. When I want to avoid caffeine, I make my tea with dried citrus fruit and fresh herbs. The flavor combination below is my favorite, but feel free to switch up the fruit and herbs to your liking.

The best way to slice the fruit is using a mandoline. It really produces very thin slices that stay intact. If you have a supersharp knife, you can use that instead.

1 blood orange

1 navel orange

1 lemon

1 lime

Sprigs of fresh thyme

Honey

Fresh lemon juice

Preheat the oven to 200°F. Using a mandoline or very sharp knife, thinly slice the citrus fruit and discard the seeds. Spread the slices on a nonreactive wire rack that fits inside a baking sheet. You want the fruit to be on the rack to allow air circulation around the whole slice.

Bake the fruit for 2 hours, flip, and then bake the other side for 1 to 2 hours more. When done, the fruit should be slightly tacky, but the rinds should be crispy and dry. Store the fruit in an airtight container for up to 7 days.

To make tea, bring water to a boil. Place a few slices of fruit in each cup, and add a sprig of fresh thyme. Pour the boiling water over the fruit and thyme; allow to steep for at least 10 minutes. Remove the fruit, and add honey and lemon juice to taste.

GREEN JUICE
(that you actually want to drink)

I was tempted to call this hangover juice. I make this simple two-ingredient drink anytime I feel a little off. Or anytime I can't remember the last time I ate a vegetable. Juicing has become so complicated these days, but start here: just two ingredients — fresh pineapple and as much kale as you can tolerate.

Yield • **Makes 2 servings**

½ fresh pineapple, peeled, top removed

3 to 6 fresh kale leaves

Push the pineapple (core and all) through a juicer slowly.

Feed the kale leaves (including their stems) through the juicer.

Stir and serve.

>>·LUNCH·<<

Apricot-Pecan
Chicken Salad
77

Warm Spinach Bacon
Mushroom Salad
78

Chicken Caesar Salad
*(with Esther's egg-free
Caesar dressing)*
81

Spinach-Artichoke
Dip-Stuffed
Portobellos
82

Cheesy Spring Risotto
85

Charred Corn Tilapia
86

Cilantro-Lime Rice
87

French Onion Soup
89

Smoky Black Bean Soup
90

Creamy Tomato Soup
Mugs
93

Cheese-Crusted
Grilled Cheese
(oh yeah!)
94

Alabama Fried Chicken
Sandwiches
96

Pimiento Grilled
Cheese . . .
with fried pickles
101

APRICOT-PECAN CHICKEN SALAD

I shouldn't divulge how many nights I've spent digging on the Internet for Central Market's apricot chicken salad recipe. Central Market is a great grocery store in Texas, if you didn't know. Its premade items have a cult following, and this chicken salad tops the list. The recipe remains top secret, but I think I've figured it out for you here.

Yield • 2 cups

½ **pound raw chicken tenders**

1 **tablespoon whole-grain mustard**

1 **tablespoon honey**

3 **tablespoon mayonnaise**

6 **dried apricots, sliced**

¼ **cup chopped pecan halves, toasted**

1 **scallion, thinly sliced**

¼ **teaspoon salt**

Freshly ground black pepper

Crackers or toast points, for serving

In a small pan, cover the chicken with water and poach for about 5 minutes, until cooked through (the internal temperature should reach 165°F). Let cool to room temperature, and then use two forks to shred.

In a medium-size bowl, whisk together the mustard, honey, and mayonnaise. Add the apricots, pecans, scallion, salt, and pepper. Taste and adjust for salt, if desired.

Serve with crackers or on toast points.

WARM SPINACH BACON MUSHROOM SALAD

This salad is everything I love for lunch, but don't often make for myself. When your job consists of recipe testing, often your entire kitchen is covered in dishes before noon. Pulling out another skillet to make a warm salad just doesn't feel right. But on the weekends, I'm all too eager to make this meal for a light Saturday lunch.

Don't miss the steps for perfect hard-boiled eggs!

Yield • Makes 2 servings

2 large eggs

4 slices bacon, chopped

5 or 6 white button mushrooms

1 tablespoon red wine vinegar

1 teaspoon honey

½ teaspoon Dijon mustard

⅛ teaspoon salt

Freshly ground black pepper

4 ounces fresh baby spinach, washed

1 scallion, sliced

Place the eggs in a small saucepan, and cover with cool water. Bring to a rolling boil over high heat. Once boiling, turn off the heat, cover the pan, and set a timer for 10 minutes. After 10 minutes, drain the eggs and peel them under cold, running water. Set aside.

Place the chopped bacon in a small skillet over medium heat. Cook, stirring occasionally, until the bacon is almost crispy—it will crisp as it cools.

Remove the bacon with a slotted spoon and set aside.

Pour off 2 tablespoons of the bacon grease into a large salad bowl.

Return the pan to the heat, and add the sliced mushrooms. Cook until nicely golden brown.

To the salad bowl with the bacon grease, add the vinegar, honey, Dijon, salt, and pepper to taste. Whisk very well to combine. Add the spinach and toss well. Scatter the bacon pieces, mushrooms, and scallion over the top and toss very well.

Slice the hard-boiled eggs. Divide the salad between two plates, and top with the sliced eggs.

CHICKEN CAESAR SALAD (WITH ESTHER'S EGG-FREE CAESAR DRESSING)

I told y'all about my best friend Esther in my first cookbook. She's back again with this super-easy recipe for egg-free Caesar dressing! After eating it at her house once, I immediately asked for the recipe and have been making it ever since. It's super-quick to throw together, and it's a dead ringer for the more complicated Caesar that requires an egg yolk.

Yield • Makes 2 servings

1 tablespoon neutral-flavored oil

2 boneless, skinless chicken cutlets (4 to 6 ounces each)

Salt

Freshly ground black pepper

½ head of romaine lettuce (chopped)

Parmesan cheese, for serving (optional)

FOR THE DRESSING
¼ cup mayonnaise

¼ cup grated Parmesan cheese

1 clove garlic, grated on a Microplane or very finely minced

1 to 2 tablespoons fresh lemon juice

Freshly ground black pepper

Pour the oil into an 8-inch nonstick sauté pan, and heat over medium heat. When the oil shimmers and is hot, sprinkle the chicken cutlets with salt and pepper, and place in the pan. Cook on one side until golden brown, about 2 minutes, and then repeat on the other side. Test the chicken with an instant-read thermometer to ensure it reaches 165°F in the thickest part. Transfer to a plate and let cool.

TO MAKE THE DRESSING: Combine all the dressing ingredients. Taste and add more lemon juice, if desired.

Combine the lettuce with the dressing and toss well until combined. Slice the chicken, scatter it on top, and top with more Parmesan, if desired. Serve.

SPINACH-ARTICHOKE DIP—STUFFED PORTOBELLOS

You know how you go to a restaurant and want to make a meal out of just appetizers? This recipe satisfies all those cravings for me. I love to order stuffed mushrooms, and I can never turn down a warm dip, especially spinach-artichoke dip! I combined the two together, and I think they make a very nice couple.

Yield • Makes 2 servings

½ teaspoon neutral-flavored oil

1 ½ cups packed raw baby spinach

1 (6-ounce) can marinated artichoke hearts

2 ounces softened cream cheese

2 tablespoons mayonnaise

3 tablespoons grated Parmesan cheese

¼ teaspoon garlic powder

Pinch of red pepper flakes

2 large portobello mushrooms

1 clove garlic, cut in half

¼ cup shredded mozzarella cheese

Preheat the oven to 350°F.

In a small skillet, heat the oil over medium heat. Add the spinach and sauté for 2 to 3 minutes, or until wilted. Drain the artichoke hearts and add them to the skillet. Sauté for 1 minute or so, just to combine, and then remove from the heat. Set the skillet aside, but do not wipe it out—you will need it again.

Combine the sautéed spinach and artichokes in a bowl with the cream cheese, mayonnaise, Parmesan, garlic powder, and red pepper flakes. Taste and add salt if you like, but I find it doesn't need it.

Wipe the portobellos with a damp cloth, and use a spoon to remove the stem and gills from underneath the mushroom. Rub the mushrooms all over with the split raw garlic clove and then place them gills up in the same skillet that the spinach and artichokes were sautéed in. Turn the heat back on to medium and sauté for 4 to 5 minutes on the first side. They should brown slightly and release some liquid. Flip the mushrooms and sauté for 2 to 3 minutes on the gills side. Remove from the heat and pat dry.

Stuff the mushrooms with the spinach-artichoke mixture, top with the mozzarella, and then bake on a greased sheet pan for 15 minutes. Serve hot.

I'll let you in on a little secret with risotto: You don't really have to stir it the entire time. I know Italian grandmothers want to throw tomatoes at me right now for saying that, but after nearly a decade of making the dish, it's just as creamy if I stir it occasionally while it cooks. That said, I set this recipe up so that all of the prep work is done ahead of time, so your hands will be free during the cooking process, should you feel the need to stir constantly. I like to use my free hand to drink the rest of the wine, but I'll let you decide.

>>·CHEESY SPRING RISOTTO

Yield • Makes 2 servings

2 cups chicken stock

1 cup water

½ pound asparagus spears, trimmed

½ cup fresh peas

1 tablespoon olive oil

2 tablespoons unsalted butter, divided

1 small onion, finely diced

1 clove garlic, minced

1 cup arborio rice

¾ cup dry white wine

¼ teaspoon salt

Freshly ground black pepper

¼ cup grated Parmesan cheese

In a 2-quart saucepan, combine the chicken stock and water. Bring to a simmer.

Slice the trimmed asparagus spears into 1-inch pieces and set aside.

Once the chicken stock is simmering, carefully submerge the asparagus in the stock for about 1 minute, to cook lightly. Remove with a strainer and transfer to a small bowl. Repeat with the peas, and add to the same bowl after cooking. Keep the stock warm over low heat.

In a 4-quart saucepan, preferably one with a heavy bottom for even cooking, combine the olive oil and 1 tablespoon of the butter. Melt over medium heat.

Add the onion and cook for 4 minutes, until translucent. Stir in the garlic and cook until fragrant, about 30 seconds.

Stir in the arborio rice. Cook, stirring frequently, for about 4 minutes, until you can see the edges of the rice grains starting to turn translucent. Then, pour in the wine, and cook until almost evaporated.

Begin adding the warm stock ½ cup at a time. Stir when you add the stock and stir again occasionally during the 5 minutes or so that it takes to absorb all the stock. Keep adding the stock in ½-cup increments until it's all gone, and keep stirring occasionally.

Stir in the salt and pepper to taste, and taste to see whether the rice is cooked through. If so, turn off the heat, and stir in the remaining tablespoon of butter, and the Parmesan and vegetables.

Divide between two bowls and serve.

CHARRED CORN TILAPIA

I owe a big hat tip to Rachael Ray for this recipe. Well, I owe her my entire hat because when I was in college, I would watch her and Giada cook on the Food Network almost every day after class. These women opened my mind on how to cook. Sure, I grew up around all the great cooks in my family, but there was just something so approachable about Rachael and Giada that made me want to get in the kitchen and cook up something new instead of study for midterms. This easy fish recipe has been one of my go-to meals for years. It's great on a bed of Cilantro-Lime Rice.

Yield • Makes 2 servings

2 tablespoons mayonnaise

1 teaspoon chili powder

2 frozen tilapia fillets, thawed

¾ cup frozen corn, thawed

Lime wedges, for serving

Preheat the broiler to high. Ensure the top rack of the oven is about 6 inches from the flame of the broiler.

Line a small sheet pan with foil, or have your broiler pan ready.

In a small bowl, combine the mayonnaise and chili powder. Smear on both sides of the fish.

Press the corn on the top side of each fillet—it will stick to the mayonnaise mixture.

Place the fish on the prepared pan, and broil for about 10 minutes. The fish will be cooked through (flaky) and white, and the corn will have charred in several places. Serve hot with lime wedges.

CILANTRO-LIME RICE

This small batch of rice is great underneath any type of protein for dinner, or even with a fried egg on top for breakfast! If you use brown rice, the cooking time will be closer to fifty minutes; white rice cooks in just twenty.

Yield • Makes 2 servings

1 cup uncooked brown or white rice, rinsed

2 cups water

1 tablespoon unsalted butter

½ teaspoon salt

1 tablespoon fresh lime juice

Handful of fresh cilantro, chopped

Combine the rice, water, butter, and salt in a medium-size saucepan with a tight-fitting lid. Bring to a boil, turn the heat to low, cover, and cook for 45 minutes for brown rice, 20 minutes for white rice. Once done cooking, turn off the heat, lift the lid on the pot, and place a clean towel loosely over the top of the pan. Place the lid back on and let it rest for 10 minutes.

Finally, stir the lime juice and cilantro into the hot rice. Serve immediately.

FRENCH ONION SOUP

You've probably already guessed as much, but I'm a real soup girl. Scaling down one of my favorites, French onion, was a delicious adventure in the kitchen for me. Traditional French onion soup uses wine to deglaze the pan of onions, but I can hardly keep a bottle of wine open long enough to cook with it. Oh, you too? Let's use whiskey instead.

One of the benefits of this scaled-down version of soup is that the onions don't take quite as long to caramelize. In this case, just 25 minutes.

Yield • 2 bowls

3 tablespoons unsalted butter

2 medium-size onions, thinly sliced

1 ½ teaspoons granulated sugar

2 tablespoons whiskey

1 tablespoon all-purpose flour

2 ½ cups beef stock

2 teaspoons soy sauce

2 teaspoons Worcestershire sauce

Salt

Freshly ground black pepper

4 slices French bread

4 slices melting cheese
(such as Swiss or Gouda)

In a 4-quart soup pot with a heavy bottom, melt the butter over medium-low heat.

Add the onions and sugar. Stir to combine, and then cook over medium-low heat, stirring occasionally, until the onions turn golden brown, about 25 minutes.

Add the whiskey to the pan and use a wooden spoon to scrape up any golden bits stuck to the bottom of the pan. Cook for 1 minute.

Stir in the beef stock, soy sauce, and Worcestershire sauce. Bring the soup to a simmer, then add salt and pepper to taste. Simmer the soup for another 10 minutes.

Divide the soup between two oven-safe bowls. Top each bowl with two slices of French bread and two slices of cheese. Melt under a broiler on low until the cheese is bubbling. Serve immediately.

SMOKY BLACK BEAN SOUP

My intention is for this recipe to be something you throw together with ingredients you already have in your pantry. It is highly adaptable: I always have a tube of tomato paste in my fridge, but I don't always have an 8-ounce can of diced tomatoes; they are interchangeable here. Lacking a fresh jalapeño? Stir in some cayenne pepper to taste. Is the cilantro in your fridge wilted? Totally fine — just use ground coriander (it's the same plant). It's pretty hard to mess up this soup. Plus, anything garnished with sour cream and crushed tortilla chips always turns out delicious.

Yield • 2 bowls

1 ½ teaspoons olive oil

1 small onion, chopped

1 jalapeño chile, finely diced

2 tablespoons tomato paste

2 cloves garlic, minced

¾ teaspoon ground cumin

1 (15-ounce) can black beans, not drained or rinsed

1 cup vegetable stock

2 scallions, sliced

Handful of fresh cilantro, chopped

Sour cream, for garnish

Tortilla chips, for garnish

Place the oil in a 4-quart soup pot and turn the heat to medium. Stir in the onion and jalapeño, and cook until translucent and starting to brown on the edges, about 5 minutes.

Stir in the tomato paste and cook, stirring, until evenly distributed. Stir in the garlic and cook for 30 seconds.

Stir in the cumin, black beans with the liquid from the can, and vegetable stock. Bring to a simmer while stirring occasionally. Let the soup simmer for 5 to 10 minutes.

Stir in the scallions and cilantro just before serving. Garnish with sour cream and crushed tortilla chips.

TIP *I call for small onions in all my recipes, but have you seen the onions in the grocery store these days? They can be the size of softballs! In that case, I would use part of the onion and wrap up the rest for another recipe. However, I recently discovered that onions sold in the mesh bags in 3- to 5-pound quantities are typically smaller. They're much more "for two"–friendly.*

CREAMY TOMATO SOUP MUGS

Soup with lunch every day is a must in my house — even in the summer. I love a good mug of soup to sip on while my lunch comes together. Creamy tomato soup made with just one can of tomatoes from the pantry is always on the menu!

Yield • 2 mugs

1 tablespoon unsalted butter

½ small onion, diced

1 clove garlic, minced

1 tablespoon tomato paste

1 (14-ounce) can diced tomatoes

2 tablespoons white wine

½ cup vegetable stock

¼ teaspoon dried basil

⅛ teaspoon salt

Freshly ground black pepper

¼ cup heavy whipping cream

In a 2-quart saucepan with a lid, melt the butter over medium heat. Stir in the onion, and cook until translucent.

Stir in the garlic and cook until fragrant, about 30 seconds.

Add the tomato paste, and cook, stirring, until dissolved.

Add the diced tomatoes, wine, vegetable stock, basil, salt, and pepper to taste, and bring to a simmer. Lower the heat, cover the pan, and let simmer for 10 minutes.

Using an immersion blender, puree the mixture in the pan. Alternatively, you can transfer the soup to a regular blender in small batches and blend carefully — be sure to crack open the blender on the top to allow steam to escape.

Just before serving, stir in the cream.

CHEESE-CRUSTED GRILLED CHEESE (OH YEAH!)

Yeah, I went there. I couldn't cram enough cheese *into* my grilled cheese, so I had to put cheese on the outside, too.

Yield • 2 sandwiches

1 tablespoon unsalted butter

1 large egg, beaten

½ cup grated Parmesan cheese

4 slices of bread

1 cup shredded melting cheese (I prefer Gouda or a mixture of cheeses)

In a 10-inch nonstick skillet, let the butter melt over medium-low heat.

Meanwhile, have the egg ready in a small bowl. Spread the Parmesan on a plate.

Brush two slices of the bread with egg, and then press each side into the Parmesan. Transfer the two slices of bread to the skillet. Cook until the cheese browns. Flip the slices, and add half of the melting cheese to one slice. Top one of the pieces of grilled bread with the other grilled bread slice (toasted side down, on top of the cheese), and continue to grill until the cheese melts, flipping as needed.

Repeat with the remaining bread and cheese to make two sandwiches. Serve immediately.

ALABAMA FRIED CHICKEN SANDWICHES

Back to our Great Southern Road Trip (a.k.a. our honeymoon):
I knew I wanted to take my husband to Birmingham, Alabama.
I had spent some time there at a Southern food writers/
photographers conference a few years back and was completely
charmed by "the Magic City." We took the recommendation
of *Southern Living* magazine, and stopped at Saw's Soul Food
Kitchen for lunch. It is, hands down, the best food I've ever had
in my life. Since then, we've been back a handful of times, always
taking the long way home for the holidays to sneak in a trip
to Saw's. On our first visit, my husband had a sweet tea fried
chicken sandwich topped with Alabama white barbecue sauce
and pickles. I had the grilled pimiento cheese with fried pickles,
plus many bites of his fried chicken sandwich! (Turn the page for
my rendition of their pimiento cheese sandwich.) If you ever find
yourself in Birmingham, please, go to Saw's. You won't regret it.

Yield • Makes 2 servings

2 boneless chicken thighs (with skin)

Salt and freshly ground black pepper

½ cup buttermilk

1 ½ cups frying oil (I use peanut)

½ cup all-purpose flour

2 hamburger buns

Leaf lettuce, for serving

Dill pickles, for serving

Lay the chicken flat in a dish, sprinkle with salt and pepper, and pour the buttermilk on top. The chicken will only be partially submerged in the buttermilk, and that's fine. Place the chicken back in the fridge while you prep for the rest of the meal. The longer it marinates the better, but a quick 15-minute marinade is just fine, too. Flip the chicken once while marinating.

TO MAKE THE SAUCE: Whisk together all the sauce ingredients. Cover and place in the fridge.

Heat the oil in a large stockpot. We are shallow frying, so the oil will not cover the chicken completely.

Place the flour in a shallow dish. Sprinkle two big pinches of salt and one pinch of pepper into the flour and mix well.

When the oil is hot (350°F), and a few pieces of flour dropped in immediately sizzle, it's time to fry!

FOR THE ALABAMA WHITE SAUCE

½ cup mayonnaise

½ teaspoon salt

1½ teaspoons freshly ground black pepper

¼ teaspoon garlic powder

Pinch of cayenne pepper

1 tablespoon white vinegar

1 tablespoon fresh lemon juice

1 tablespoon granulated sugar

Take the chicken out of the buttermilk, and dredge it in the flour. Use your fingers to press as much flour into the surface as possible. Using tongs, carefully lower the chicken, skin side down, into the oil. Fry on the first side until golden brown, and then flip once. Cook the second side until golden brown. Check the temperature of the chicken with an instant-read thermometer to ensure it reaches 165°F in the thickest part.

Split the hamburger buns and toast them lightly. Top the buns with a generous dose of the white sauce, lettuce, pickles, and fried chicken. Enjoy!

TIP *If you can only find chicken thighs with the bones in them, buy them, and cut the bones out with sharp kitchen scissors. It's easier than it sounds, I promise.*

I don't know if I've talked enough about how much I love the great state of Alabama. At yet another trip to Saw's (see my Alabama Fried Chicken Sandwiches on page 96 for an explanation), I ordered a grilled pimiento cheese with fried pickles. I swear, when I walked into the restaurant, the words *pimiento grilled cheese* were glowing on the chalkboard menu. I didn't even look at the rest of the menu; I just ordered. And I didn't even think twice to share a bite with my husband, either.

I love this recipe because even if you don't want to grill it, you still get a small batch of pimiento cheese. I make pimiento cheese as a quick snack on the weekends frequently. But when I really want something special, I spread it between two thick slices of bread and grill it. And I top it with fried pickles.

PIMIENTO GRILLED CHEESE . . .
with fried pickles!

Yield • 2 sandwiches

FOR THE FRIED PICKLES
12 dill pickle slices

¼ cup cornmeal

¼ cup all-purpose flour

¼ teaspoon garlic powder

¼ teaspoon freshly ground black pepper

3 tablespoons buttermilk

1 ½ cups neutral-flavored oil (I use peanut)

TO MAKE THE PICKLES: Heat the oil in a small but deep pot or a skillet. Clamp a thermometer to the pan, and let the oil heat to 375°F.

Meanwhile, dry the pickles very well with paper towels.

In a small bowl, combine the cornmeal, flour, garlic powder, and black pepper. Place the buttermilk in another small bowl.

When the oil has reached 375°F, bread the pickles by dipping them in the buttermilk, then the cornmeal mixture. Fry four at a time, removing them from the oil when they are golden brown and crispy, about 90 seconds.

Let the fried pickles drain on a paper towel.

FOR THE PIMIENTO CHEESE

½ cup mayonnaise

2 tablespoons diced jarred pimientos

½ teaspoon Worcestershire sauce

½ teaspoon freshly grated onion

Pinch of cayenne pepper

1 cup shredded Cheddar cheese

1 cup shredded sharp Cheddar cheese

1 tablespoon unsalted butter,
for grilling

4 slices thick bread

TO MAKE THE PIMIENTO CHEESE: Combine all the ingredients, except the bread and butter, and stir well.

Melt the butter over medium heat in a skillet large enough to fit all the bread slices. Toast the bread on one side, flip, and divide the pimiento cheese mixture between two slices. Stack the remaining bread slices on top of the pimiento cheese, and flip and grill until both sides are golden brown.

Serve the pimiento grilled cheese stacked high with fried pickles.

DINNER

≫·PERFECT FILETS MIGNONS

Nothing says "date night dinner" to me more than two petite filets mignons. This cut of meat is so tender and perfect, it hardly needs a thing done to it. So, this is more a method than a recipe. Most steak houses get a quick sear on the steaks and then finish them in the oven. That's exactly what we're going to do here, and we're going to have perfectly cooked steaks!

Yield • Makes 2 servings

2 (4- to 6-ounce) filets mignons

1 teaspoon granulated sugar

1 teaspoon salt, plus more for sprinkling

½ teaspoon coarsely ground black pepper

1 tablespoon high-heat oil (such as canola)

For even cooking, be sure your filets are at room temperature before proceeding. This helps prevent the "charred on the outside, rare on the inside" problem most people have when cooking steaks.

Preheat the oven to 350°F.

Combine the sugar, salt, and pepper in a small dish. Rub the outside of each filet with the spice rub.

Place the oil to a medium-size cast-iron skillet. Preheat the skillet over high heat until you can hold your hand about 4 inches from the surface for only a few seconds. Lower the heat to medium-low, then add the steaks.

Cook the steaks for 4 to 6 minutes on each side. Do not touch or move the steaks while they sear.

Slide the skillet into the preheated oven and bake the steaks until they are 5°F lower than your ideal temperature range. For medium rare, that's 140°F.

Carefully remove the steaks from the oven, wrap in foil, and let rest for 10 minutes.

Serve the steaks with an extra sprinkle of salt on top.

TIP *What's with the sugar? Sugar helps the caramelization process. You won't taste anything sweet, but your steaks will have a lovely dark crust.*

≫ TWICE-BAKED POTATOES

The heartiest, happiest side dish in all the lands. I make these more often than I should, but they're just so delicious!

Yield • Makes 2 servings

2 large russet potatoes, scrubbed clean

3 slices bacon

¼ cup sour cream

1 tablespoon milk

1 tablespoon unsalted butter

½ cup shredded Cheddar cheese

¼ teaspoon salt

Freshly ground black pepper

1 scallion, sliced

Preheat the oven to 400°F.

Place the potatoes directly on the oven rack and roast for 60 minutes, flipping every 20 minutes. Alternatively, you could cook them in the microwave much faster—6 to 8 minutes on high, flipping halfway through.

While the potatoes cook, cook the bacon in a skillet until almost crisp. Remove it from the pan, and it will crisp as it cools. Chop the bacon.

When the potatoes are done, remove them from the oven and let rest until cool enough to handle. Turn the oven temperature down to 350°F.

Slice the potatoes in half, and scoop out most of the flesh, but leave a ¼-inch border to hold their shape.

Mash the potato flesh with the bacon, sour cream, milk, butter, cheese, salt, pepper, and scallion. Scoop this mixture back into the awaiting potato skins. Place on a baking sheet, and bake for 10 to 15 minutes, until the cheese melts.

FESTIVE GRILLED HAM
with Brian's Corn Casserole and Perfect Collard Greens

While it definitely makes me sad when we have to celebrate Easter without family, it does happen. Word of advice: Don't move too far away from home. Ever. But my husband and I still try to have all of our Easter favorites. Instead of a giant ham, I reach for thick-sliced ham steaks. So much easier! And if you like that popular store-bought ham with a sweet glaze (you know the one), try brushing the ham steaks with apricot or apple jelly right when they come out of the pan.

Corn casserole is another must for us (at any holiday, really), and although my husband was dubious of the need to scale this one down because he loves it so, even he can admit a 9 × 13-inch pan of any casserole is too much. I use a mini oval casserole dish that is about 8 × 6 inches and holds 2 cups of water to the top.

As for a small batch of collard greens, well, those are just the way to my heart. Instead of filling your washing machine with greens (like many Southern cooks do when they're serving a crowd), this batch just fills your sink. Well-cooked greens are ethereal and silky. Try this recipe — you just might become a greens lover!

Yield • Makes 2 servings

CORN CASSEROLE

½ cup finely ground cornmeal

2 teaspoons granulated sugar

½ teaspoon baking powder

¼ teaspoon baking soda

¼ teaspoon salt

½ cup sour cream

1 (8.25-ounce) can creamed corn

1 (8.75-ounce) can corn kernels, drained and rinsed

2 tablespoons unsalted butter, melted

PERFECT COLLARD GREENS

6 large collard green leaves (the size of dinner plates)

4 slices bacon, diced

1 jalapeño chile, minced

2 tablespoons cider vinegar

½ cup water

½ teaspoon salt

½ teaspoon freshly ground black pepper

HAM STEAKS

Cooking spray

4 thick-sliced ham steaks

¼ cup apricot jam (optional)

TO MAKE THE CORN CASSEROLE: Preheat the oven to 350°F, and have ready a mini casserole dish that roughly measures 8 × 6 inches and holds 2 cups of water to the brim.

In a small bowl, whisk together the cornmeal, sugar, baking powder, baking soda, and salt.

Stir in the sour cream, creamed corn, and corn kernels. Stir very well.

Pour the mixture into the casserole dish. Pour the melted butter evenly over the surface.

Bake for 35 to 38 minutes, until the surface is starting to turn golden brown in places. Serve warm.

TO MAKE THE COLLARD GREENS: Wash the greens very well in the sink—they often have a lot of sand in them. Be thorough.

Remove and discard the stem from each leaf. Slice the leaves in half where the stem used to be, and then stack them all together. Beginning at the shorter end, roll up the leaves into a cigar shape. Slice into ½-inch-thick ribbons.

Place the diced bacon in a 2-quart saucepan, and turn the heat to medium. Cook the bacon until it releases its fat and is starting to crisp. Remove it from the pan with a slotted spoon and set aside.

Add the greens to the pan along with the jalapeño. Sauté for about 5 minutes, until the greens start to wilt. Then, stir in the vinegar, water, salt, and pepper. Lower the heat and let the greens gently simmer, covered, for 35 to 40 minutes. Taste before serving—they should be silky, smoky, and tangy all at once.

MAKE THE HAM STEAKS: When the corn and greens are nearly ready, heat a large grill pan over high heat until you can only hold your hand a few inches above the surface for a few seconds. Spray it lightly with cooking spray, and place the ham steaks in the pan—do not move them for at least 1 minute, to form grill marks. Flip them and repeat on the other side. If you want a sweet glaze on the ham, warm the jam in a microwave and brush it on the steaks when they come out of the pan.

THANKSGIVING DINNER FOR TWO

Apple-Molasses-Glazed Turkey, Southern Corn Bread Dressing, Crazy Good Sweet Potatoes, and a Small Batch of Cranberry Sauce

I'm not suggesting you avoid your family for the holidays and celebrate with just the two of you. Sometimes it sounds like a good idea, but really, having a family that drives you crazy is good for you. It actually makes you less crazy. Trust me. I've proven this. I use these recipes for a small Thanksgiving dinner in July. Or February. Or anytime I crave the flavors of the holiday but am months away from November.

First up: Let's talk turkey. You are either a white meat or dark meat kind of a gal (or guy). Pick what you like and go with it. Grocery stores are selling cut-up turkey more and more these days. I frequently see boneless turkey tenderloins. That's what I've used here. Now, I'm a dark turkey meat kind of a gal. I'm the only one in my family who feels this way, so I get the entire leg and wings on Thanksgiving Day. It's glorious. But, for this recipe, you can use turkey drumsticks. They will take longer to cook, but just use a meat thermometer, and you'll be fine.

We probably should have talked about the dressing first. This corn bread dressing is famous in my family. My parents make a big deal out of Thanksgiving every year, and between my dad's staying up all night to smoke the turkeys and my mom's famous corn bread dressing, people drive from hours away to attend their Thanksgiving dinners. This recipe is the one you must make from this book, if nothing else!

My favorite part of the meal is sweet potatoes. I bake them until they're tender and oozing their sweet sugary syrup, and then top them with my homemade marshmallows. You can absolutely substitute store-bought marshmallows. I just like the way homemade marshmallows melt and form a solid layer of crunchy fluff. But mini marshmallows are way easier. It's your choice. If I'm really going all out, I'll round this meal out with Easy Stovetop Mac 'n Cheese (page 140) or Baked Mac 'n Cheese (page 139), Brian's Corn Casserole (page 111), and Perfect Collard Greens (page 111).

Apple-Molasses—Glazed Turkey Tenderloin

Yield • Makes 2 servings

FOR THE TURKEY
6 cups cold water

2 bay leaves, crushed

5 black peppercorns

1 tablespoon salt

¼ cup light brown sugar

1 turkey breast tenderloin
(roughly 1 pound)

3 stalks celery

FOR THE GLAZE
½ cup apple jelly

2 tablespoons molasses

TO BRINE THE TURKEY: Whisk the water with the bay leaves, peppercorns, salt, and brown sugar, and place in a medium-size bowl.

Add the turkey tenderloin. Poke it in several places with a fork to help the brine soak in.

Let brine overnight, at least 8 hours.

The next day, preheat the oven to 400°F.

Chop the celery stalks into three pieces, and line the bottom of an 8-inch square baking dish with it. This is the bed for the turkey to bake on.

Remove the turkey from the brine and dry it thoroughly. Place the turkey on the celery.

TO MAKE THE GLAZE: Microwave the apple jelly and molasses in a small dish in the microwave on high for 30 to 45 seconds. Stir to melt completely.

Brush a thick layer of apple jelly mixture onto the turkey, and slide it into the oven. Roast for 33 to 35 minutes total, brushing on more glaze every 10 minutes. An instant-read thermometer inserted in the thickest part of the meat should register 165°F.

You can cook the dressing while the turkey cooks.

Southern Corn Bread Dressing

Cooking spray

6 corn muffins (page 171, but subtract 1 tablespoon of sugar from the recipe)

2 slices white bread

¾ teaspoon salt

Freshly ground black pepper

¾ teaspoon dried rubbed sage

1 teaspoon dried poultry seasoning

3 tablespoons unsalted butter

⅓ cup water

⅓ cup chopped celery

⅓ cup chopped onion

1 large egg

¾ cup chicken stock

¼ cup milk

Preheat the oven to 400°F, and spray with cooking spray a mini casserole dish that holds 2 cups of liquid.

In a medium-size bowl, crumble the corn muffins into fine crumbs. Do the same for the white bread, though a few chunks of white bread are fine. Add the seasonings to the mixture, and spread the mixture on a baking sheet. Toast in the oven until the breads feel dried out, about 10 minutes, stirring once halfway through. Let cool on the counter before pouring back into the bowl.

Meanwhile, in a 2-quart saucepan, combine the butter, water, celery, and onion. Cook over medium heat until the onion and celery soften, about 5 minutes, stirring occasionally.

Add the cooked vegetables to the bread mixture, and stir in the egg, chicken stock, and milk until homogeneous. Pour the mixture into the baking dish. Resist the urge to smooth the surface—a rough surface encourages crisp brown pieces (which are delicious!).

Bake for 20 minutes. Let cool for 10 minutes before slicing and serving.

Crazy Good Sweet Potatoes

2 large sweet potatoes

3 tablespoons light brown sugar

½ teaspoon ground cinnamon

1 batch homemade marshmallows (page 202), or ½ cup store-bought mini marshmallows

Bake the sweet potatoes in the 400°F oven with the turkey and dressing, until the insides are soft, about 40 minutes, depending on the size of your sweet potatoes.

Remove the sweet potatoes from the oven, slice in half, and remove all the flesh, leaving a ¼-inch border around the edges to hold everything together.

To the sweet potato flesh in a bowl, mash in the brown sugar and cinnamon. Divide the mixture among the sweet potato skins.

Top with as many homemade or store-bought marshmallows as you like, and torch with a kitchen torch to toast the marshmallows.

A Small Batch of Cranberry Sauce

1 cup fresh cranberries

3 tablespoons granulated sugar

1 tablespoon water

Fresh orange zest (optional)

Combine all the ingredients, including the orange zest, if using, in a small saucepan, and cook over medium heat until the berries begin to burst.

Pour into a serving dish, and serve.

APPLE CIDER–GLAZED CHICKEN BREASTS WITH PAN-GLAZED CARROTS

Chicken breasts are such versatile dinners for two. I love this recipe because the marinade and glaze is one and the same — we soak the chicken breasts in a sweet, spicy apple cider mixture, and then use that same marinade to pan-glaze the carrots later on. It's a meal all made in the same skillet, which is all I can usually manage to pull together for weeknight suppers.

Yield • Makes 2 servings

2 boneless chicken breasts (with skin)

2 cups apple cider

4 whole peppercorns

2 small bunches of fresh sage, torn and chopped

½ teaspoon salt

2 tablespoons olive oil

Salt and freshly ground black pepper

4 carrots, peeled and sliced into sticks

1 tablespoon unsalted butter

Most likely, your chicken breast still has the tenderloin attached (it's the extra piece that looks like a chicken finger). Remove it. This helps the chicken cook faster. I freeze the tenderloins for soup or make chicken fingers with them.

In a large pan or bowl, combine the chicken, apple cider, peppercorns, sage, and ½ teaspoon of salt. Let marinate, covered, in the fridge for a minimum of 4 hours.

After 4 hours, remove the chicken (but save the marinade) and pat the chicken dry. Heat the oil in a large skillet (I don't recommend nonstick, for better browning). When the oil is hot, sprinkle the chicken with extra salt and pepper and place it skin side down in the pan. Cook on both sides until golden brown.

Place the carrots in a microwave-safe bowl, cover with plastic wrap, and microwave for 1 minute on high.

Once both sides of the chicken are golden brown, strain and discard the peppercorns and sage from the apple cider marinade. Pour it over the chicken. Adjust the heat so the apple cider comes to a simmer, and cook until the chicken registers 165°F on an instant-read thermometer, 5 to 7 minutes. Remove the chicken from the pan and set aside when done.

Once the chicken is done, turn the heat to high and reduce the apple cider to a thick glaze, about 5 minutes. Add the carrots and sauté for 3 to 4 minutes, until crisp-tender. Add the butter before removing them from the pan. Stir to coat the carrots in the glaze and butter.

Use any extra glaze from the pan to brush on the chicken.

Serve the chicken with the carrots.

SWEET TEA FRIED CHICKEN

My love letter to the South.

Toss the chicken in the marinade Friday night, then fry the bird after church on Sunday. You can use store-bought sweet tea, or make your own (see tip).

Yield • Makes 2 servings

1 ½ cups sweet tea

1 bone-in chicken breast (with skin), chopped in half through the bone

2 or 3 chicken drumsticks (with skin)

1 cup buttermilk

1 tablespoon + 1 teaspoon salt, divided

4 tablespoons unsalted butter

2 tablespoons oil
(I use peanut oil)

1 ½ cups all-purpose flour

1 teaspoon freshly ground black pepper

TIP *To make the sweet tea, steep two black tea bags in 1 ½ cups of hot water and add 2 tablespoons of sugar after the tea bags are removed.*

First, boil the sweet tea in a pan until it reduces to ½ cup. Let cool completely.

Place the chicken pieces in a medium-size bowl. In a small glass, whisk together the buttermilk, sweet tea, and the 1 tablespoon of salt. Stir well to dissolve the salt. Pour this mixture over the chicken, cover, and marinate for 48 hours.

When ready to cook, preheat the oven to 425°F.

When the oven is at temperature, place the cast-iron skillet on the center rack and let it heat for 10 minutes. Place the butter and oil in the hot pan. It should melt almost immediately and begin to sizzle. Place the pan back in the oven.

Bread your chicken. Remove the pieces from the marinade, but reserve the marinade. Add the wet pieces of chicken to the flour mixture and use your hands to toss, to coat each with the flour mixture. Then, repeat the process: back into the marinade again and then the flour mixture to coat. You have just double-battered the chicken!

Carefully arrange the chicken pieces in the hot pan. The chicken should immediately start to sizzle and cook. Return the pan to the oven and bake for 20 minutes.

Flip the chicken, place it back in the oven, and then bake for another 14–18 minutes. Test the chicken with an instant-read thermometer: it should read 165°F in the thickest part of the meat and the juices should run clear.

Immediately remove the chicken from the skillet and let cool for 10 to 15 minutes. Serve warm.

I am a big fan of sheet pan suppers. Not only are they superfast to throw together while the oven preheats, but minimal dish cleanup is the way to my heart. I make a lot of versions of this meal, with both pork tenderloin and a regular pork roast. If you use a pork tenderloin, it will cook in much less time than will a standard pork roast. No matter which cut of meat I use, I try to keep it at 1 pound to 1 ½ pounds maximum. This helps the meat and vegetables cook at a similar rate. If you use a pork roast on the larger side, you may need to remove the vegetables while it finishes cooking. Keep them covered while the pork finishes cooking, and everything will stay warm for dinnertime.

I'm giving you two different marinade options here. Each marinade recipe makes enough for both the pork and leeks. Also, feel free to substitute any vegetables that you prefer.

SHEET PAN SUPPER: ROASTED PORK and LEEKS

Yield • Makes 2 servings

MARINADE #1

¼ cup Dijon mustard

¼ cup honey

2 cloves garlic, minced

1 lemon, sliced in half

6 tablespoons olive oil

1 teaspoon salt

Freshly ground black pepper

MARINADE #2

¼ cup balsamic vinegar

2 cloves garlic, minced

6 tablespoons olive oil

2 tablespoons dried rosemary

1 teaspoon salt

Freshly ground black pepper

1 (1- to 1 ½-pound) pork tenderloin or pork roast

3 leeks

You can do this the night before or in the morning before work. Make the marinade of your choice by combining all its ingredients in a bowl. Place the pork in a dish or a large resealable plastic bag, and pour half of the marinade over it. Cover the pork and marinate it in the fridge for as long as you can — up to 8 hours. At the same time, cover and refrigerate the unused marinade.

Preheat the oven to 450°F, and line a large sheet pan with foil.

Trim the leeks and remove all of the green tops — only the white part is edible. Rinse very well in cold water, and pat dry. Slice the leeks in half and toss with the reserved portion of marinade. Place on the prepared sheet pan.

Add the pork (with all of its marinade) to the sheet pan, and bake for 20 minutes. Test the temperature of the pork and monitor the browning of the leeks.

Remove the pork from the oven when it is 140°F. Transfer the vegetables to a serving bowl, and tent the foil over the pork while it rests and comes to 145°F. Let it rest for 15 minutes before slicing and serving with the leeks.

TIPS: *I save the green part of the leeks to make vegetable or chicken broth.*

I buy single pork tenderloins from my butcher, but if your bag comes with two, either scale up the recipe to serve more, or place one in the freezer for a future sheet pan supper.

SHEET PAN SUPPER: SWEET and SPICY ASIAN SALMON WITH CABBAGE STEAKS

Another easy, healthy meal—slide in the oven and get on with your life! I use half of the sweet and spicy glaze before roasting, and I use the other half to brush on top after the oven. Serve the salmon on top of the cabbage steaks, or dice up the cabbage to make a bed for the salmon to rest on — your choice!

Yield • Makes 2 servings

2 (6-ounce) salmon fillets

1 small head green cabbage

2 tablespoons light brown sugar

2 tablespoons soy sauce

1 tablespoon rice vinegar

1 tablespoon sesame oil

2 cloves garlic, minced or grated on a Microplane

1 (1-inch) piece fresh ginger, minced or grated on a Microplane

½ teaspoon red pepper flakes

1 scallion, sliced, for serving

Preheat the oven to 400°F, and line a rimmed sheet pan with foil.

Place the salmon on the foil. Slice ½-inch "steaks" from the head of cabbage. Reserve the rest of the cabbage for another use.

In a small bowl, whisk together the brown sugar, soy, vinegar, sesame oil, garlic, ginger, and red pepper flakes. Pour half on the salmon and cabbage, coating very well.

Bake for 20 minutes, until the salmon is flaky and the cabbage is tender.

Brush the remaining glaze on top and serve.

SHRIMP 'N GRITS

Ahhh, shrimp and grits. I could never tire of this meal. Where I'm from, grits are always savory, never sweet. I especially love grits with lots of spicy heat. I use a jalapeño for spice in the shrimp, but you can amp up the heat even more with hot sauce on top.

Yield • Makes 2 servings

FOR THE SHRIMP
1 tablespoon neutral-flavored oil

1 small onion, diced

1 celery stalk, diced

1 small green bell pepper, diced

1 small jalapeño chile, minced

3 cloves garlic

2 tablespoons tomato paste

½ pound shrimp
(I use 21–25/pound size)

Pinch of salt

Freshly ground black pepper

FOR THE GRITS
1 cup milk

1 cup water

½ cup instant stone-ground grits

¼ teaspoon salt

¼ teaspoon garlic powder

Freshly ground black pepper

1 cup shredded Cheddar cheese

1 tablespoon unsalted butter

TO MAKE THE SHRIMP: Place the oil in a 10-inch skillet, and turn the heat to medium-high. When the oil shimmers and is hot, add the diced onion, celery, bell pepper, and jalapeño. Sauté until the onion is translucent and the peppers soften. Stir in the garlic and cook until fragrant, about 30 seconds. Next, stir in the tomato paste and a pinch of salt and black pepper.

Push the vegetable mixture to the edges of the pan, and add the shrimp to the middle of the pan. Sprinkle with a pinch of salt and pepper, and let cook undisturbed on the first side until a nice crust is formed, about 1 minute. Flip the shrimp and cook the other side for 1 minute. The shrimp should be done at this point. Turn off heat and cover to keep warm while making the grits.

TO MAKE THE GRITS: In a 2-quart saucepan, bring the milk and water to a boil, then slowly whisk in the grits, about 1 tablespoon at a time, while vigorously whisking. Once the grits thicken and come up to a bubble, stir in the salt, garlic powder and black pepper. Continue cooking the grits until all the liquid is absorbed. Turn off the heat, and stir in the cheese and butter.

Divide the grits between two bowls, and top with the shrimp mixture.

There is no denying my love of New Orleans and Creole food. I didn't come across a single gumbo that I didn't love on my last trip to New Orleans. Gumbo can be made with all different types of meat, but this is my favorite version: chicken, shrimp, and sausage. Gumbo typically takes hours to prepare, but *Southern Living* magazine shared a secret time-saving step a few years ago that I use frequently in my kitchen: pretoasting the flour. Instead of waiting for the roux to turn a copper color, you can save time by starting with golden brown flour. It just takes a few minutes to do in a skillet. Make a large batch and save it for anytime you need a golden roux, or make just what you need for this small pot of gumbo.

GLORIOUS GUMBO

Yield • Makes 2 servings

¼ cup all-purpose flour

¼ cup vegetable oil

½ cup chopped onion

½ cup chopped celery

½ cup seeded and chopped green bell pepper

6 ounces smoked sausage (such as kielbasa)

3 cups boiling water

2 tablespoons powdered beef bouillon

⅛ teaspoon cayenne pepper

¼ teaspoon freshly ground black pepper

½ teaspoon dried thyme

1 tablespoon Worcestershire sauce

8-ounce can diced tomatoes

1 bay leaf

1 chicken breast

1 cup sliced okra, fresh or frozen and thawed

5 ounces shrimp (21–25/pound), deveined, tails removed

⅓ cup fresh parsley, chopped

Cooked white rice, hot, for serving

Preheat the oven to 400°F.

Spread the flour evenly in a small cast-iron or other oven-proof skillet and toast it in the oven for 20 minutes, stirring every 5 minutes. It will change color to a light brown. Let it cool completely before using.

In a medium-size stockpot, heat the oil over medium-high heat. Add the toasted flour and cook for about 10 minutes, stirring almost constantly. The mixture should be a copper penny color before you move on to the next step. Don't take it too far or it can burn.

Add the onion, celery, bell pepper, and sausage. Sauté for 5 to 7 minutes, stirring occasionally. The onion should soften and the sausage should brown a bit.

Add the water, beef bouillon, cayenne and black pepper, Worcestershire sauce, tomatoes, and bay leaf.

Bring to a simmer, cover and turn the heat to low. Cook for 45 minutes.

Add the chicken breast whole and cook, uncovered, for 20 minutes. When the chicken is done, remove it from the pot, shred the meat, then add it back to the pan. Add the okra, and cook, uncovered, for 5 minutes.

Right before serving, add the shrimp and parsley, and cook for 4 to 5 minutes, until the shrimp are done. Serve over white rice.

Anytime COMFORT FOODS

>>·≪ ... ·≪

CHICKEN 'N DUMPLINS

Where I'm from, dumplins aren't pronounced dumplinGs, and they are actually big, flat noodles. If you come from the land of puffy, biscuit dumplings, I'm so sorry to disappoint you here! But I have a hunch you can use my buttermilk biscuit recipe (page 39) for your dumplings successfully. In that case, I'd add a bit more buttermilk to the biscuit recipe to make the dough thinner before adding to the soup.

To make a small batch of homemade chicken stock, I grab those packages of half-chickens at the store. A package usually has one thigh, one drumstick, and one breast with bones and skin. Sometimes, I've had to buy a whole cut-up chicken, but in that case, I freeze half of it. However, I also want to say that if you want to use a quart of store-bought stock and precooked chicken with this recipe, that is totally fine. Just make sure to make your dumplins from scratch so you can take all the credit.

Yield • 2 big bowls

FOR THE CHICKEN
1 half-chicken with bones and skin
(1 breast, 1 drumstick, 1 thigh)

6 cups water

1 bay leaf

Freshly ground black pepper

Salt

2 tablespoons unsalted butter,
at room temperature

2 tablespoons all-purpose flour

TO MAKE THE CHICKEN: In a 2-quart heavy saucepan, place the raw chicken, water, bay leaf, and pepper. Bring to a boil over medium heat, then lower the heat and simmer, uncovered, until the chicken registers 165°F in the thickest part of the breast. It should take about 45 minutes.

Strain the chicken pieces out of the broth, and return it to the stove. You should have 4 cups of broth. Add a few pinches of salt, and taste for saltiness. Adjust the salt according to how salty your mama made chicken soup when you were growing up.

Let the chicken meat rest on the counter until cool enough to handle. Then, shred the meat, removing all skin and bones as you go.

Meanwhile, bring the stock to a boil. In a small bowl, mash the butter and flour together with a fork. Try to make the mixture homogeneous, and then stir it into the boiling broth. The broth should thicken slightly from the roux. Let the mixture simmer away while you prepare the dumplins.

FOR THE DUMPLINS

¾ cup all-purpose flour,
plus more for rolling

¼ teaspoon baking powder

⅛ teaspoon salt

2 tablespoon unsalted butter

¼ cup milk

TO MAKE THE DUMPLINS: Stir the flour, baking powder, and salt together in a small bowl. Work the butter into the mixture using your fingertips. You want little bits of butter spread throughout the flour, almost like you're making biscuits. Finally, stream in the milk and stir until the dough comes together.

Flour a surface and rolling pin very well, and then roll out the dough until ⅛ inch thick. It will be a rough 8-inch circle. Using a pizza cutter, slice the dumplings into flat noodles, for a total of eighteen to twenty noodles.

Transfer the dumplins to the simmering broth, and cook for 3 to 4 minutes, until done. Add the shredded chicken back to the pot, and serve immediately.

BAKED CHICKEN FINGERS

You need this recipe in your arsenal. Sure, kids like it, but the secret truth is that adults love it, too. I frequently triple the recipe for Game Day, and they're always gone by half-time. I coat mine in cornflakes because that's what my mom used when I was growing up. They're extra crunchy and extra delicious.

Yield • Makes 2 servings

2 cups cornflakes

½ teaspoon seasoned salt or regular salt

¼ teaspoon freshly ground black pepper

¼ teaspoon garlic powder

¼ teaspoon onion powder

1 large egg

¼ cup milk

1 pound chicken tenders

Cooking spray, for pan

Preheat the oven to 350°F.

In a large resealable plastic bag, combine the cornflakes, seasoned salt, pepper, garlic powder, and onion powder. Crush the cornflakes and spices with your hands or a mallet.

In a small, shallow bowl, beat the egg and milk together.

Dip each chicken tender in the egg mixture, and then drop it into the bag with the cornflakes. Shake to coat each chicken tender with the cornflake mixture.

Spray a wire rack with cooking spray, and then place each chicken tender on top. Fit the wire rack on top a baking sheet.

Bake for 25 minutes.

Serve the chicken fingers with your desired dipping sauces.

BAKED MAC 'N CHEESE

Yes, I really have two recipes for mac 'n cheese. This recipe is the baked version that's more familiar for Sundays. I make the stovetop version on page 140 for weeknight meals or lunches. This baked version is a classic. But I made it even easier — instead of combining everything on the stove first and making a roux, it all goes in the blender! You can have classic baked mac 'n cheese without all the extra dishes. Yay!

P.S. Don't forget the onion powder. It makes a big difference here.

Yield • 2 ramekins

1 cup dried macaroni

1 cup milk

2 tablespoons all-purpose flour

½ teaspoon onion powder

¼ teaspoon salt

2 cup grated Cheddar cheese

⅔ cup bread crumbs

2 tablespoons unsalted butter, melted

Preheat the oven to 350°F. Have ready two 10-ounce ramekins on a baking sheet.

Bring a medium-size pot of water to a boil. Cook the macaroni in the boiling water for about 4 minutes (it should still have a bite in the middle.) Drain the pasta. Don't overcook it because it will continue to cook in the oven.

Meanwhile, in a blender, combine the milk, flour, onion powder, and salt and blend well. Once the pasta is done, pour it into a bowl and add the milk mixture and Cheddar. Stir to combine. Divide the mixture between the two ramekins (it will seem like there's too much liquid, but you're okay). Sprinkle half of the bread crumbs over each ramekin and drizzle the butter evenly on top. Bake on a sheet pan for 45 minutes. Let cool for 5 minutes before serving.

EASY STOVETOP MAC 'N CHEESE

This recipe is a little too easy — I'm tempted to make it several times a week in the winter to stay warm. Most macaroni and cheese recipes require a roux for thickening, but in this case, I've bypassed that step by whisking the flour directly into the milk before heating it. It makes this already easy dish even easier. And cheesier. Speaking of cheese, I like to grate my own. It melts the quickest that way.

Yield • Makes 2 servings

1 ½ cups dried elbow macaroni

¾ cup + 2 tablespoons milk, divided

1 tablespoon all-purpose flour

1 cup freshly grated Muenster cheese

¼ cup freshly grated sharp Cheddar cheese

Salt

Freshly ground black pepper

In a 2-quart saucepan, bring plenty of water to a boil for cooking the macaroni. Once boiling, add a big pinch of salt, and cook the macaroni according to the package directions. Drain and set the same pot back on the stove.

Lower the heat under the pot to medium, and add ¾ cup of the milk.

In a small dish, vigorously whisk together the remaining 2 tablespoons of milk and the flour.

Once the milk is simmering in the pan, add the flour mixture. Bring to a simmer again.

Add the grated cheeses to the pot, and stir until melted.

Finally, pour the macaroni back into the pot. Taste and add salt and pepper to your liking.

EASIEST CHICKEN POTPIE

And I mean the absolute easiest! I make the creamy chicken filling for a chicken potpie in about 15 minutes in a skillet, and then I pour it over toast. We miss out on the mess on making piecrust, but we still get all the creamy, comforting flavors of chicken potpie. I just don't know if I can make potpies any other way now.

Yield • Makes 2 servings

2 tablespoons unsalted butter, divided

½ pound raw chicken tenders, diced

1 small onion, diced

1 small carrot, peeled and diced

¼ cup frozen peas

¼ cup frozen corn

¼ teaspoon dried thyme leaves

2 tablespoons all-purpose flour

2 tablespoons heavy whipping cream

1 cup milk

Salt

Freshly ground black pepper

2 slices thick bread

In a small skillet, melt 1 tablespoon of the butter over medium heat. Add the diced chicken tenders to the skillet along with a pinch of salt and pepper. Cook until the chicken is browned on both sides, about 4 minutes per side. Transfer the chicken from the pan to a plate, and try to leave as much butter in the pan as possible.

Add the remaining tablespoon of butter to the pan, along with the onion and carrot. Sauté until the onion is translucent and the carrot begins to soften, about 5 minutes.

Add the peas and corn to the skillet. Crush the thyme leaves with your fingers to release the oils as you add them to the pan.

Stir in the flour, and let cook for 1 minute.

Add the cream and milk to the pan and stir and cook until thickened, 1 to 2 minutes. The mixture should come to a gentle simmer.

Taste for salt and pepper, and adjust accordingly.

Meanwhile, toast the bread, and slice in half, placing two halves on each plate. Top with the warm chicken mixture and serve.

CHICKEN PARMESAN FOR TWO

I've probably spent too much time trying to decipher the best bread crumb topping for these chicken breasts. You would be surprised what was voted #1 in a blind test — onion hamburger buns. It sounds kind of random, but when you cook for two, you always have excess hamburger buns in your freezer. I saw the big flecks of onion on top of the buns, and gave it a whirl in the food processor. No one was more surprised than me when they were picked as the favorite. So, that said, you can use any fresh bread here, but my pick for ultimate flavor is hamburger buns with big pieces of caramelized onions on top. The bakery in your grocery store should carry them.

Yield • Makes 2 servings

FOR THE SAUCE

1 (14-ounce) can whole tomatoes in tomato juice

2 cloves garlic, grated on a Microplane or finely minced

½ teaspoon dried oregano

1 teaspoon granulated sugar

¼ teaspoon salt

Freshly ground black pepper

1 tablespoon grated Parmesan cheese

TO MAKE THE SAUCE: Combine all the ingredients, except the Parmesan, in a 1-quart saucepan, and bring to a boil. Lower the heat slightly, and let simmer briskly until reduced by half. You will end up with about ⅔ cup of sauce. Stir in the Parmesan.

TO MAKE THE REST: Bring a large pot of water to boil for the spaghetti. Salt the water generously before adding the pasta and cooking it per the directions on the box.

Pour the olive oil into a 10-inch skillet, and turn the heat to medium-high.

Process the hamburger buns in a food processor until soft crumbs form. Place the crumbs in a shallow dish.

Line up another shallow dish with the flour. Line up a third shallow dish with the beaten egg.

Sprinkle salt and pepper on each side of the chicken breasts.

FOR THE REST

4 ounces uncooked spaghetti

Salt

Freshly ground black pepper

¼ cup olive oil, for frying

2 onion-flecked soft hamburger buns

¼ cup all-purpose flour

1 large egg, beaten

2 (6- to 8-ounce) boneless, skinless chicken breasts

4 thick slices of fresh mozzarella cheese

Dip the chicken breasts into the flour, and dust them off gently to give them a light coating of flour.

Dip the chicken breasts in the egg, followed by the bread crumbs.

Once the oil is hot, carefully add the chicken breasts. Let them cook undisturbed on the first side until a golden brown crust forms, about 5 minutes. Flip the chicken breasts and cook all the way through, another 5 minutes or so. Use a meat thermometer to ensure the temperature in the thickest part is 165°F.

To serve, toss the spaghetti with almost all of the sauce, and place the chicken breasts on top. Add the reserved sauce on top of the chicken breasts, followed by two slices of mozzarella on each. The residual heat of the chicken will melt the cheese.

POP-ABLE TURKEY MEATBALLS

What makes these meatballs so pop-able? A little cube of cheese stuffed inside! This recipe makes ten meatballs, but can easily be scaled up for your next party. Make it easy on yourself and use store-bought pasta sauce for the base. I take the cheesiness up another level by using three-cheese pasta sauce.

Yield • 10 meatballs

Cooking spray

1 cup store-bought pasta sauce

½ pound lean ground turkey

2 cloves garlic, minced or grated on a Microplane

1 large egg yolk

½ teaspoon dried basil

⅓ cup dried bread crumbs

⅛ teaspoon salt

Freshly ground black pepper

10 (¼-inch) cheese cubes of your choice (I used a firm cheese, such as aged Cheddar)

Preheat the oven to 375°F, and spray an 8-inch square baking dish lightly with cooking spray.

Pour the pasta sauce in the bottom of the prepared baking dish.

In a medium-size bowl, combine the ground turkey with the garlic, egg yolk, basil, bread crumbs, salt, and pepper. Mix the mixture very well with your hands, but also be careful not to over-mix and make tough meatballs.

Take a level tablespoon of dough, press a cheese chunk in the middle, and top with another level tablespoon of dough. Roll in your hands gently to make a ball. Place each ball in the baking dish. Repeat to use up all turkey mixture and cheese cubes.

Bake for 20 minutes. Serve immediately.

I hail from the land of "Mexican food at all hours of the day," also known as Texas. Mexican food for dinner always has a way of turning any Tuesday into a fiesta. When I found out my daughter's due date was one day after Cinco de Mayo, all I could think about was whether or not she'd come early so I could enjoy a margarita . . . and whether or not I could fit a sombrero in my hospital bag.

Mexican food is an integral part of every Texan's life. Texans may move to another state, but rest assured, they will never move to a state without a great Mexican restaurant nearby. But since it always tastes best in Texas, as soon as they set foot back in Texas, their first meal is always Mexican food.

That's a lot of prep for me to say when I make enchiladas, they are fantastic. My mom makes a fabulous light chicken version with a sour cream sauce, but what I really crave is "the red ones": meaty steak tossed with roasted green chiles, too much cheese, all smothered with a homemade enchilada sauce made with the best chile powder you can find (I swear by Gebhardt's).

➤➤· BEEF ENCHILADAS

Yield • 4 enchiladas

**FOR THE HOMEMADE
ENCHILADA SAUCE**

2 tablespoons unsalted butter

2 tablespoons neutral-flavored oil

3 tablespoons all-purpose flour

2 tablespoons tomato paste

2 heaped tablespoons chile powder

½ teaspoon ground cumin

½ teaspoon onion powder

¼ teaspoon garlic powder

¼ teaspoon salt

¼ teaspoon freshly ground
black pepper

Pinch of cayenne pepper

2 cups chicken stock

2 teaspoons white vinegar

FOR THE ENCHILADAS

1 (8-ounce) steak, cooked to medium,
diced

1 (4-ounce) can green chiles

4 (8-inch) flour tortillas

2 cups shredded Cheddar cheese

Sour cream, for serving
(optional)

Pickled jalapeños, for serving
(optional)

Preheat the oven to 400°F, and have an 8-inch square baking dish nearby.

TO MAKE THE ENCHILADA SAUCE: In a 2-quart saucepan, melt the butter and oil over medium heat.

Whisk in the flour, and cook until it turns a lightly golden color.

Whisk in the tomato paste and all the spices. Cook for 1 minute, until fragrant. Slowly pour in the chicken stock and bring to a simmer. Let the mixture simmer for about 5 minutes to thicken.

Remove from the heat, and stir in the vinegar.

TO MAKE THE ENCHILADAS: In a medium-size bowl, stir together the diced steak, green chiles, and ½ cup of the enchilada sauce.

Taking one tortilla at a time, place one-quarter of the sliced steak mixture slightly to the left of center, top with 2–3 tablespoons of cheese, and then roll up to close. Place seam side down in the baking dish. Repeat with the remaining tortillas.

Top with remaining enchilada sauce and cheese. Bake for 20 minutes.

Serve with sour cream and pickled jalapeños, if desired.

ONE-SKILLET BEEF AND CHEDDAR PASTA

I want to brag on my mom for a quick second. My mom has always worked full-time, and yet I always came home to homemade dinners. Not only did she make me the type of woman who will always want to work and set goals for myself, but she reminds me that it can be done all while eating well, too. So, that said, I've never had the boxed version of this dish. But this homemade version is absolutely delicious and oh-so-craveable in the winter.

Yield • 2 bowls

2 teaspoons neutral-flavored oil

½ pound lean ground beef (I use 93% lean)

1 ¼ cups milk

¾ cup water

1 cup uncooked elbow macaroni

1 tablespoon cornstarch

2 teaspoons chili powder

1 teaspoon garlic powder

½ teaspoon salt

1 teaspoon smoked paprika

Pinch of cayenne pepper (optional)

1 cup shredded Cheddar cheese

In a 10-inch skillet, heat the oil until shimmering and hot. Add the ground beef and cook, breaking it up into small chunks with a wooden spoon as you go. Once the beef is cooked all the way, tilt the pan slightly and use a paper towel to soak up any extra grease.

Heat the milk and water together in a 2-cup measuring cup in the microwave for about 45 seconds, until hot. Add this to the beef mixture, along with the macaroni.

Stir in all the remaining ingredients, except the cheese, and bring the mixture to a simmer. Lower the heat to low, and cover the pan. Cook for 10 minutes, checking on it after 5 minutes. Give it a quick stir, and if the mixture seems to be sticking to the pan, stir very well and add a splash more water.

After 10 minutes, taste the macaroni and check for doneness. If done, stir in the cheese and divide between two bowls before serving.

MEAT LOAF . . .
that you actually crave

When I set out to create meat loaf for two, I knew I wanted a fresher, healthier take on it. I know how lucky I am that I didn't grow up on the typical greasy, heavy meat loaf; my mom only made meat loaf with ground turkey. She is still testing new recipes for it to this day, and it seems that each new recipe has more and more vegetables packed into it. This version is my homage to hers: it's made with ground turkey, packed with carrots, and covered in a tangy glaze that no one can resist.

Yield • 2 mini loaves

FOR THE GLAZE
¼ cup ketchup

1 tablespoon balsamic vinegar

½ teaspoon freshly ground black pepper

Preheat the oven to 350°F.

TO MAKE THE GLAZE: In a small bowl, whisk together all the glaze ingredients. Set aside.

FOR THE MEAT LOAF

¾ pound ground turkey

½ cup freshly shredded carrot

1 tablespoon Worcestershire sauce

1 teaspoon dried Italian seasoning

½ teaspoon salt

Freshly ground black pepper

1 large egg yolk

½ cup fresh bread crumbs
(1 slice bread, ground in
a food processor)

3 teaspoons neutral-
flavored oil, divided

½ small onion, finely diced

2 cloves garlic, minced

TO MAKE THE MEAT LOAF: In a medium-size bowl, combine the turkey, carrot, seasonings, egg yolk, and bread crumbs. Use your hands to combine the mixture very well.

In an 8-inch oven-proof skillet, heat 2 teaspoons of the oil over medium-high heat. Sauté the onion until the edges are beginning to turn golden, about 4 minutes, then add the garlic and cook for another minute. Scrape this mixture into the turkey mixture. Mix well to combine.

Divide the turkey mixture in half, and shape into two mini loaves. Meanwhile, heat the remaining 1 teaspoon of oil in the same skillet that you cooked the onion and garlic in, and place the meat loaves bottom side down in the pan (this helps retain the loaf shape). Cook on the first side until browned, about 2 minutes, and then flip gently and sear the top side. Finally, smear with half of the glaze and transfer the skillet to the oven. Cook for 10 minutes, top with the rest of the glaze, and then cook for an additional 10 minutes. Test the meat loaf to ensure it's done—it should register 165°F on an instant-read thermometer before you remove it from the oven.

TIPS: *I'm a stickler about grated carrots—they must be freshly grated. The grated carrots sold in bags at the grocery store are dry and often cut too large to fully melt into a dish. One medium-size carrot equals ½ cup shredded.*

Use it up: If you don't buy your ground turkey directly from the butcher and request exactly ¾ pound, you will find that most packages of ground turkey have 1 pound of meat. Simply wrap the excess ¼ pound and store in the freezer, or use it in my Green Chile Chili (page 168) or One-Skillet Beef and Cheddar Pasta (page 150).

JALAPEÑO POPPER MASHED POTATOES

My love affair with jalapeños goes about as deep as you would expect for a Texan. We pack jalapeños into our salsas, we stuff them with cheese and deep-fry them, and we even stuff pickled ones with peanut butter. (Don't ask about that last one.) But chopped up and folded into cheesy mashed potatoes just might be my favorite way to eat 'em.

Yield • Makes 2 servings

2 small russet potatoes (12 ounces total weight)

¾ teaspoon salt, divided

1 ½ tablespoons unsalted butter

¼ cup half-and-half, milk, or cream

1 small jalapeño chile, minced

½ cup shredded white Cheddar cheese

Freshly ground black pepper

Peel and chop the potatoes into equal-size pieces.

In a 2-quart saucepan, place the potato pieces and ½ teaspoon of the salt, and cover with cold water by 2 inches or so.

Turn the heat to high, and bring the potatoes to a boil. Lower the heat to a simmer, and cook the potatoes until they fall off a knife and are tender all the way through, about 15 minutes.

Drain the potatoes, and place them back in the same pot you cooked them in. Add the remaining ¼ teaspoon of salt and the butter, half-and-half, jalapeño, cheese, and pepper to taste. Mash the potatoes in the pan, and serve hot.

POTATO CHIP-CRUSTED PORK CHOPS

I specifically designed this recipe to use the amount of potato chips in one bag . . . minus a few handfuls for snacking. So, I buy the 8-ounce bag (not the family size), munch on a few, and then crush it up for my favorite pork chop coating. After a quick bake in the oven, you have crispy-crunchy chops!

This is one of those recipes where I just don't know how many chops you consider a serving size. I can eat one chop, but my husband can eat two. So, I usually cook four chops total, and I have one left over for lunch the next day. But if you are a one-chop person, then cut the recipe in half (and enjoy the other half of that bag of chips!).

Yield • 4 pork chops

Cooking spray

2 large eggs

1 ½ cups crushed potato chips
(about 7 ounces)

4 boneless thin pork chops

Preheat the oven to 375°F; line a baking sheet with foil and spray lightly with cooking spray.

In a small, shallow bowl, beat the eggs together. In another shallow bowl, place the crushed potato chips.

Dip each chop in the egg, followed by the potato chips, then place on the prepared baking sheet.

Bake for 12 minutes, flip the chops, and bake for another 12 minutes. Before removing from the oven, test the chops for doneness, because cooking times vary due to thickness.

CLASSIC LASAGNE

A date night pleasing meal if there ever was one. If you're double-dating, double the recipe and make an 8-inch pan of lasagne. Triple dating, or serving a crowd? Double it again and make a 9 × 13-inch dish. You've got lots of options with this lasagne.

Yield • 2 large pieces

Cooking spray

FOR THE MEAT SAUCE
1 tablespoon olive oil

1 small onion, diced

2 cloves garlic, minced

2 tablespoons tomato paste

1 teaspoon Italian seasoning

½ teaspoon dried oregano

8 ounces ground beef

1 (14-ounce) can crushed tomatoes

2 tablespoons red wine

¼ teaspoon salt

Freshly ground black pepper

FOR THE REST
8 ounces fresh ricotta cheese

½ teaspoon salt

Freshly ground black pepper

1 large egg, beaten

6 tablespoons grated Parmesan cheese, divided

5 ounces shredded mozzarella cheese (about 1 cup)

4 no-cook flat lasagna noodles

First, lightly spray a 9 × 5 × 3-inch loaf pan with cooking spray, and preheat the oven to 400°F.

TO MAKE THE MEAT SAUCE: In a medium-size skillet over medium-high heat, sauté the onion in the olive oil. Cook until the edges of the onion start to caramelize. Stir in the garlic and cook for 30 seconds. Stir in the tomato paste and dried herbs, and cook until fragrant, about 1 minute.

Push everything in the skillet to the edges of the pan, and add the ground beef in the middle. Cook while breaking up with a wooden spoon. Sauté the beef until nicely golden brown.

Stir in the crushed tomatoes, wine, salt, and pepper to taste. Let simmer for 10 to 15 minutes.

TO MAKE THE REST: Meanwhile, in a bowl, stir together the ricotta, salt, pepper, egg, and 3 tablespoons of the Parmesan.

Spread ½ cup of the meat sauce in the prepared pan. Place a lasagna noodle on top. Top the noodle with one third of the ricotta mixture. Sprinkle over one-third of the mozzarella cheese. Repeat twice. The final layer should be the last lasagna noodle followed by the last of the meat sauce. Top everything with the remaining 3 tablespoons of Parmesan.

Cover the pan with foil, and bake for 30 minutes, removing the foil at the 25-minute point to let the cheese brown. The sauce should be bubbling hot. Let cool in the pan for 15 minutes before attempting to slice and serve.

SPINACH LASAGNE ROLL-UPS

Another fun way to scale down lasagne and prevent the "leftovers for days" scenario. I layer my mom's recipe for spinach lasagne onto the actual noodles, roll them up, and bake! Each little roll-up is just a few bites of lasagne, so plan on two or three per person. You may substitute 2 cups of your favorite store-bought sauce instead of using my sauce recipe.

Yield • Makes 2 servings (6 rolls)

FOR THE SAUCE

1 (14-ounce) can whole tomatoes in tomato juice

2 cloves garlic, grated on a Microplane or finely minced

½ teaspoon dried oregano

1 teaspoon granulated sugar

¼ teaspoon salt

Freshly ground black pepper

1 tablespoon grated Parmesan cheese

TO MAKE THE SAUCE: If you're making the sauce from scratch, combine all the sauce ingredients in a small saucepan and simmer, uncovered, for 20 minutes, stirring occasionally.

TO MAKE THE LASAGNE: Preheat the oven to 350°F and grease a medium-size baking dish with the olive oil.

Cook the lasagna noodles in boiling water until al dente, about 1 minute under the time recommended on your box. Remove from the water, lay them out between two paper towels, and keep covered.

Take the spinach (it really must be thawed!) and use your hands to squeeze out the excess liquid. Give it a few good squeezes—it should appear mostly dry when you're done.

In a small bowl, stir together the spinach, ricotta, egg, red pepper flakes, nutmeg, salt, and black pepper. Mix well.

FOR THE LASAGNE

1 tablespoon olive oil

6 wavy lasagna noodles
(not the no-boil kind)

8 ounces frozen chopped spinach, thawed

8 ounces ricotta cheese

1 large egg

¼ teaspoon red pepper flakes

¼ teaspoon freshly grated nutmeg

½ teaspoon salt

¼ teaspoon freshly ground pepper

8 ounces fresh mozzarella cheese, grated

6 tablespoons freshly grated
Parmesan cheese

Take one lasagna noodle and evenly spread one-sixth of the cheese mixture on it (see photo), then top with grated mozzarella. Roll up the noodle away from you, starting at a short end. Place it seam side down in the prepared baking dish. Repeat for the remaining five noodles.

Pour the tomato sauce on top and sprinkle with any remaining mozzarella. Sprinkle 1 tablespoon of Parmesan over each roll-up.

Bake for 25 minutes, until the sauce is bubbly and the cheese is melted. Serve.

TUNA NOODLE CASSEROLE

Maybe this dish was a little overdone when I was growing up. But, that doesn't mean we can't enjoy a homemade version of it! I take the extra time to make a white sauce from scratch rather than relying on a condensed soup, and I really think that's what makes this mini casserole for two so great.

Yield ● Makes 2 servings

FOR THE SAUCE

2 tablespoons unsalted butter

2 tablespoons all-purpose flour

1 cup milk

¼ cup heavy whipping cream

½ teaspoon salt

¼ teaspoon freshly ground
black pepper

⅛ teaspoon freshly grated nutmeg

FOR THE FILLING

2 cups dried egg noodles

1 teaspoon neutral-flavored oil

½ cup diced onion

½ cup chopped white button mushrooms

½ cup sliced celery

½ cup frozen peas

⅛ teaspoon salt

⅛ teaspoon freshly ground
black pepper

⅛ teaspoon freshly grated lemon zest

1 (6-ounce) can tuna packed
in water, drained

½ cup bread crumbs

2 tablespoons unsalted butter, melted

Preheat the oven to 350°F, and have ready two small oven-proof ramekins that hold 10 ounces of liquid each.

TO MAKE THE SAUCE: Melt the butter in a 2-quart saucepan over medium-low heat. Whisk in the flour and cook for 1 minute.

Stir in the milk, cream, salt, pepper, and nutmeg. Bring to a simmer, and cook until thickened, about 3–5 minutes.

TO MAKE THE FILLING: Cook the egg noodles in plenty of salted boiling water. Drain and set aside.

Place the oil in the pot you cooked the egg noodles in. Turn the heat to medium. Add the onion, mushrooms, and celery. Sauté, stirring occasionally, for about 10 minutes, until softened. Before removing from the heat, stir in the peas, salt, pepper, and lemon zest.

Combine the sauce, cooked vegetables, tuna, and noodles in a bowl. Divide the mixture equally between the two ramekins.

Top each ramekin with half of the bread crumbs, and drizzle the melted butter on top.

Bake for 20 minutes, or until bubbling.

⋙· TACO SALAD

I don't often ask my husband, "What do you want to eat?" but when
I do, he always says, "Taco salad." I'm always happy to oblige because
this lunch is so delicious: filling yet light and full of flavor. I vary the
toppings on the salad, sometimes substituting turkey for beef, or
adding avocados and bell peppers (or whatever else helps clean out my
vegetable drawer in the fridge), but the dressing is always the same:
equal parts mayo and salsa with several dashes of chipotle hot sauce.
And if you're lucky, you might turn the page and find My Mom's Famous
Salsa Recipe to use for the dressing!

Yield • Makes 2 servings

8 ounces ground beef or turkey

1 ear of corn

2 tablespoons salsa (see My Mom's Famous Salsa Recipe, page 167)

2 tablespoons mayonnaise

4 to 5 dashes chipotle Tabasco sauce

1 small head of romaine lettuce, washed and chopped

1 cup canned black beans, drained and rinsed

½ cup shredded cheese of your choice

Tortilla chips, for garnish

Optional toppings: sour cream, more salsa, scallions, pickled jalapeños, avocado

In a nonstick skillet over medium-high heat, cook
the ground beef until done. Use a wooden spoon
to break up the clumps of meat. Drain on a paper
towel and set aside. I use an enamel-coated cast
iron skillet.

Char the corn either in the same skillet used for
the meat over high heat, or if you have a gas range,
char the corn directly in the fire. Use tongs to turn
it often. Remove from the heat and let cool before
slicing the kernels off the cob.

In a small bowl, whisk together the salsa, mayo,
and chipotle sauce. Whisk well, and set aside.

In a large salad bowl, combine the lettuce, corn
kernels, black beans, and cheese. Toss very well,
then drizzle the dressing on top. Toss again, and
divide between two plates. Serve with crushed
tortilla chips on top, and any other additional
toppings you like.

MY MOM'S FAMOUS SALSA RECIPE (you are so lucky!)

I feel like you are so lucky to receive my mom's famous salsa recipe. She has been making it for decades, and it's always the most requested recipe at any party. It has a bright, fresh taste, all the while relying on canned tomatoes, so you can make it year-round. She can't remember where she found the original recipe, though most recipes in our family start out as *Southern Living* recipes to which we put our own spin. My brother and I have altered the recipe throughout the years — he uses serranos instead of jalapeños, and I add chili powder for an extra depth of flavor.

Yield • 2 cups

1 (14-ounce) can diced tomatoes

1 to 2 jalapeño chiles

1 small purple onion

2 cloves garlic

2 tablespoons fresh lime juice

½ cup fresh cilantro (stems included)

2 teaspoons chili powder

1 teaspoon salt

Tortilla chips, for serving

First, slightly drain off some of the liquid from the canned tomatoes — just a tablespoon or two.

Pour the drained tomatoes into the bowl of a food processor.

Chop the jalapeños, removing the seeds and white veins to reduce the heat level of the salsa. Or leave them whole for an extra-spicy salsa! Add the chopped jalapeños to the food processor.

Peel and roughly chop the onion before adding it to the food processor. Add all the remaining ingredients, except the tortilla chips, and pulse until combined.

Taste the salsa with a tortilla chip to check for saltiness. If it seems to need salt, try adding more lime juice first. Always taste salsa with a chip because the chips usually have quite a bit of salt on them!

Serve with tortilla chips, or use as a salad dressing for my Taco Salad (page 164).

GREEN CHILE CHILI

I made this one night on a whim at my mother-in-law's house, and she and my sister-in-law flipped over it. The original recipe called for pulled chicken, which required an extra pot, so I made this version lunch-friendly by using ground turkey to streamline the process. The flavors are so familiar and likable, everyone will be asking you for this recipe. Feel free to use ground turkey, beef, or chicken — it all tastes good here!

Yield • 2 bowls

2 teaspoons neutral-flavored oil

½ pound ground turkey, chicken, or beef

1 small onion, diced

3 cloves garlic, minced

1 tablespoon ground cumin

½ teaspoon dried oregano

½ teaspoon salt

Freshly ground black pepper

1 (4-ounce) can fire-roasted and diced green chiles

1 (15-ounce) can white beans, drained and rinsed

2 cups chicken stock

¼ cup milk

2 tablespoons finely ground cornmeal

Sour cream, for garnish (optional)

Grated cheese, for garnish (optional)

Cilantro, for garnish (optional)

In a 2-quart soup pot, heat the oil over medium heat. Once hot, add the ground meat and cook, stirring frequently to break up any large chunks.

Once the meat is almost done cooking, add the onion and continue to cook, stirring occasionally.

Stir in the garlic, cumin, oregano, salt, and pepper. Let cook until fragrant, about 1 minute.

Stir in the chiles, beans, and chicken stock. Bring the mixture to a boil. Lower the heat to a simmer.

Whisk together the milk and cornmeal in a small bowl, then pour the mixture into the pot. Bring the mixture to a simmer and cook for 5 minutes to thicken.

Serve with your choice of garnishes, if desired.

I was a single gal living on my own for many years before I met my husband. What's a single girl to do with an entire pan of corn bread? I ended up with a lot of hunks of corn bread in my freezer. I finally got wise and scaled down a recipe to make just six corn muffins. I serve these with soup or chili, but I also use the entire batch to make my mom's famous Southern Corn Bread Dressing (page 117). In that case, I use regular yellow cornmeal, which is a great substitute for the harder-to-find blue cornmeal. I just love the pretty color of blue corn muffins, though.

A SMALL BATCH OF CORN MUFFINS

Yield • 6 muffins

½ cup stone-ground blue or yellow cornmeal

⅓ cup all-purpose flour

2 tablespoons granulated sugar

¾ teaspoon baking powder

⅛ teaspoon baking soda

¼ teaspoon salt

1 large egg

½ cup buttermilk

1 ½ tablespoons unsalted butter, melted, plus butter for serving

Preheat the oven to 400°F. Line six cups in a muffin pan with paper liners.

In a medium bowl, whisk together the cornmeal, flour, sugar, baking powder, baking soda, and salt.

In a small bowl, whisk together the egg, buttermilk, and melted butter.

Combine the wet ingredients with the dry ingredients and let set for a minute before scooping equal portions into the muffin cups and baking for 12 to 15 minutes.

The muffins are done when a toothpick inserted comes out clean. Serve immediately with extra butter.

>>· SKILLET PIZZA

When we get a craving for pizza, even the smallest take-out pizza leaves us with too many leftovers. I don't want my pizza binge to last more than one day, so I make this mini skillet pizza for two. I make the pizza dough in a measuring cup, so it's quick and easy. The pizza is baked in a 10-inch oven-safe skillet. I think you'll be surprised how easy it is to have a quick pizza at home! To make it even quicker, you can use store-bought pizza sauce; the recipe below makes enough for two pizzas — freeze the leftovers!

Yield • 1 (10-inch) pizza

FOR THE DOUGH

5 tablespoons warm water (105°–110°F)

½ teaspoon granulated sugar

½ teaspoon active dry yeast

¾ cup all-purpose flour, plus more for dusting

¼ teaspoon salt

1 tablespoon olive oil, plus more for cup

TO MAKE THE DOUGH: In a 2-cup measuring cup, combine the warm water, sugar, and yeast. Stir to dissolve. Let sit for 5 minutes, or until foamy. If the yeast does not foam, it's dead — start over.

Add the flour and stir. Then, add the salt and olive oil. Stir with a fork until a shaggy dough forms. Transfer the dough to a floured surface and knead it a few times. As soon as you start kneading, the dough will come together and lose all the stickiness. Knead for about 1 minute. The dough should be easy to work with, pliable, and not sticky. Grease the measuring cup with the extra oil, and plop the dough back into it. Turn the dough over once to coat it with oil, then let it rise in a warm place until doubled in bulk, about 1 hour. (See photo for reference.)

TO MAKE THE SAUCE: Combine all the sauce ingredients, except the Parmesan, in a 1-quart saucepan, and bring to a boil. Lower the heat slightly, and let simmer briskly until reduced by half. You will end up with about ⅔ cup of sauce. Stir in the Parmesan.

Preheat the oven to 450°F.

FOR THE SAUCE

1 (14-ounce) can whole tomatoes in tomato juice

2 cloves garlic, grated on a Microplane or finely minced

½ teaspoon dried oregano

1 teaspoon granulated sugar

¼ teaspoon salt

Freshly ground black pepper

1 tablespoon grated Parmesan cheese

FOR ASSEMBLY

1 tablespoon olive oil

1 cup shredded mozzarella cheese

Dried oregano, for topping pizza

Any pizza toppings you like: pepperoni, mushrooms, etc.

TO ASSEMBLE THE PIZZA: Brush the tablespoon of olive oil generously on a 10-inch oven-safe skillet.

Remove the dough from the measuring cup, and lightly flour a surface. Roll out and stretch the dough to about 11 inches in diameter. Fit the dough in the pan, stretching it as you go. Fold over any excess to make the edge of the crust.

Place the skillet over high heat and cook until the underside of the crust has splotches of light golden brown. Don't overcook.

Spread ⅓ cup of pizza sauce on top of the dough, and sprinkle on the cheese and any additional toppings.

Slide the skillet in the oven, and bake for 5 to 8 minutes, until the cheese is bubbling. Check the underside of the dough before removing from the oven—it should be a crisp, golden brown surface.

More
DESSERTS
≫·FOR TWO·≪

After the publishing of my first cookbook, I had the pleasure of being asked to bake a few desserts for two on the *Today Show* one morning. I was beyond excited, and chatted back and forth with the producer several times before going on air. She asked a lot of questions about the person who eats the other half of my desserts for two, and I shared the story of how I met my husband. Little did I know, that embarrassing story would be the first thing Matt Lauer said on air before my segment.

My husband had attempted to make a pecan pie cheesecake to impress me at a work party, but it was a big flop. It slid all over the plate and was raw in the middle. I still tease him about it to this day, but now, we eat this version of pecan pie cheesecake. Much better.

One more small note: I have a habit, albeit good or bad, of substituting a copious amount of bourbon for vanilla in any recipe. In the case of this pecan pie topped with brown sugar cheesecake in a vanilla wafer crust, I'm positive it's a good call.

PECAN PIE CHEESECAKE

Yield • 1 (6-inch) cheesecake

FOR THE CRUST
1 cup vanilla wafer crumbs
(about 30 cookies, crushed)

1 tablespoon light brown sugar

2 ½ tablespoons unsalted
butter, melted

FOR THE PECAN PIE FILLING
⅓ cup granulated sugar

¼ cup dark corn syrup

2 tablespoons unsalted butter

1 large egg

¾ cup chopped pecans

1 tablespoon bourbon whiskey

Preheat the oven to 350°F, and spray a 6-inch mini cheesecake springform pan with cooking spray.

TO MAKE THE CRUST: In a medium-size bowl, combine the cookie crumbs, brown sugar, and butter. Stir until well mixed. Press the crumbs firmly into the bottom of the springform pan and halfway up the sides. Bake for 8 minutes, and then remove the pan from the oven. Turn down the oven temperature to 325°F.

TO MAKE THE PECAN PIE FILLING: In a 2-quart saucepan over medium heat, combine all the ingredients for the filling, except the whiskey. Bring to a boil, lower the heat to maintain a simmer, and then simmer until thickened, 8 to 10 minutes. Just a reminder: A simmer is when small bubbles form around the edges of the pan. If you cook this mixture at anything higher, it will harden like candy.

Remove the pecan pie filling from the heat, and stir in the bourbon. Stick your head above the pan and enjoy the aroma of bourbon melting into hot sugar and butter. Kidding (kind of).

FOR THE CHEESECAKE FILLING

8 ounces cream cheese, softened

⅓ cup light brown sugar

1 tablespoon all-purpose flour

1 large egg

½ teaspoon vanilla extract

2 tablespoons unsalted butter, melted

TO MAKE THE CHEESECAKE FILLING: In a medium-size bowl, beat together all the cheesecake ingredients until very well mixed.

Pour the pecan pie mixture over the crust, followed by the cheesecake mixture. Spread the cheesecake mixture to the edges of the pan with a small spatula. Ensure the cheesecake mixture is flat and evenly distributed.

Bake the cheesecake on a small baking sheet for 35 to 41 minutes. The cheesecake is done when only the center of it lightly jiggles when gently shaken. A small amount of butter may leak outside of your springform pan, but it's fine — I've never known a springform pan not to leak. If you find one that doesn't, call me and tell me the brand!

When the cheesecake comes out of the oven, it will be slightly puffy. Place it next to the oven to cool; drastic temperature changes cause cracks in cheesecakes. Let the cheesecake cool gently. It will deflate, but it will turn into a perfectly flat cheese-cake. Place in the fridge for at least 6 hours before unmolding and serving.

TIP *People ask me all the time whether they really have to let ingredients like butter or cream cheese come to room temperature before baking. The answer is a resounding YES. I can't stress it enough. If your cream cheese is cold, it will not blend properly and you will see white chunks in your final product. To speed up the softening time, slice the cream cheese and let it sit at room temperature on a plate until it feels slightly cooler than room temperature. Your finger should easily leave an indentation. Or place it (still in the wrapper) in a bowl of warm water for a few minutes.*

I'm a firm believer that tiramisu needs to make a comeback. Not only is it easy to make, but it's no-bake, too!

What should you do with the leftover canned pumpkin? How about pumpkin spice lattes and mochas (pages 66 and 69)?

Feel free to substitute store-bought pumpkin pie spice for the homemade blend.

PUMPKIN SPICE TIRAMISU

Yield • Makes 2 servings

¾ cup boiling water

1 tablespoon (heaping) instant espresso powder

1 tablespoon dark rum

8 ounces mascarpone cheese, softened

½ cup canned pure pumpkin puree

⅔ cup + 2 tablespoons powdered sugar, divided

1 teaspoon pumpkin pie spice, plus more for dusting (recipe on page 66)

12 ladyfingers (½ package)

½ cup heavy whipping cream

If making the homemade pumpkin pie spice, combine all the spice ingredients in a jar and shake. Store in an airtight jar for up to 6 months.

In a shallow bowl, stir together the boiling water, espresso powder, and rum. Have ready a 1-quart casserole or similarly sized dish.

In a small bowl, stir together the mascarpone, pumpkin, ⅔ cup of the powdered sugar, and teaspoon of pumpkin pie spice. Set aside.

Dunk each ladyfinger in the espresso mixture, and place six of the ladyfingers in a single layer in the casserole dish.

Spread half of the pumpkin mixture on top. Repeat with the remaining ladyfingers and pumpkin filling.

Cover and chill for at least 4 hours, or overnight.

Before serving, whip together the cream and the remaining 2 tablespoons of powdered sugar. Spread on top of the tiramisu, and dust with extra pumpkin pie spice, if desired.

# APPLE SLAB PIE

When it comes to apple desserts, I take a cue from my favorite bakery,
Big Sur Bakery, and go heavy on the nutmeg, easy on the cinnamon.
Apples have enough flavor to stand on their own, and cinnamon has
a way of overpowering them. Nutmeg is the perfect complement.

A few years ago, slab pie became the new trend in pie-eating. And since
I would never want your dessert habits to be out of style, I scaled down
the slab pie to serve two. A slab pie is typically larger and flatter than
a regular pie, all the while cramming in just as much pie flavor. I think
you'll love this mini slab pie made in a loaf pan to serve two.

Yield • Makes 2 servings

FOR THE CRUST
Cooking spray

1 cup + 2 tablespoons
all-purpose flour

2 teaspoons granulated sugar

¼ teaspoon salt

5 tablespoons cold unsalted butter

½ teaspoon cider vinegar

4 to 5 tablespoons ice-cold water

FOR THE FILLING
2 medium-size Granny Smith apples

¼ cup light brown sugar

2 tablespoons granulated
sugar, plus more for top

1 tablespoon fresh lemon juice

½ teaspoon ground cinnamon,
plus more for top

½ teaspoon freshly grated nutmeg

2 tablespoons all-purpose flour

1 large egg yolk, beaten

Preheat the oven to 350°F, and lightly spray a 9 × 5 × 3-inch loaf pan with cooking spray.

TO MAKE THE CRUST: In a medium-size bowl, combine the flour, granulated sugar, and salt. Stir until combined, and then dice the cold butter before adding it to the mixture. Use your fingers or a pastry blender to blend the butter into the flour mixture until it's smaller than peas. It should clump together lightly in your hand when squeezed.

Stir the vinegar and 4 tablespoons of the water into the dough. Stir with a fork until it comes together; if it seems a bit dry, add the final tablespoon of water. Gather the dough into a ball, and press it into a flat disk on a well-floured surface. Cut it roughly in half, with one of the halves being slightly larger.

Roll the larger dough half into an 11 × 7-inch rough rectangle — about the size of the bottom of the loaf pan with an extra inch on all sides. Carefully transfer the dough to the loaf pan and press it into the bottom, but let the excess come up the sides of the pan. Don't stretch the dough up the sides of the pan; just let it naturally rest on the edges.

TO MAKE THE FILLING: Peel and slice the apples. I cut six or seven slices out of each quarter of an apple, and then cut the slices in half once to make them fit into the pan easier. Place the apples in a bowl, stir in the brown sugar, the 2 tablespoons of granulated sugar, and the lemon juice, cinnamon, and nutmeg. Stir very well and then let rest while you continue.

Roll out the other half of the dough to about the size of the loaf pan on top — an extra ½ inch around the edges is helpful for sealing.

Stir the apples again, and then stir in the flour very well. Pour the apples into the bottom crust, and top with the top crust. As best as you can, use your fingers to push the two edges of the dough together to create a light seal — don't worry too much about this part.

Brush the egg yolk on top, and sprinkle the extra granulated sugar and cinnamon on top of the dough before sliding the pan into the oven.

Bake for 45 to 50 minutes, until the edges of the dough are turning golden brown and the juices of the apples are bubbling.

Let cool completely (overnight in the fridge is best) for cutting perfect bars. If messy is your thing, just dig right in when it comes out of the oven.

EASIEST CHOCOLATE PUDDING

This dessert has a super-fancy name. It's actually *pots de crème*. But I'll translate it for you: It's chocolate pudding that doesn't require any cooking at all. It's perfection. It sets entirely in the fridge. So, while you have to wait a few hours for everything to set, at least you don't have to turn on the oven.

Since this recipe uses a raw egg yolk, make sure your eggs come from a clean, reliable source.

Yield • Makes 2 servings

5 ounces semisweet chocolate chips

⅛ teaspoon salt

2 tablespoons granulated sugar

1 large egg yolk

¾ cup heavy whipping cream

½ teaspoon vanilla extract

¼ cup very hot prepared espresso, or ¼ cup very hot water + 1 teaspoon instant espresso powder

Whipped cream, for serving

Blood orange slices, for serving (optional)

In the bowl of a food processor, combine the chocolate chips, salt, and sugar. Pulse ten to fifteen times to break up the chocolate chips. The grittiness of the sugar will help this process. Add the egg yolk and vanilla. Pulse to combine.

Warm the cream in the microwave on low until warm to the touch, about 45 seconds.

Finally, while the processor is running, stream in the hot espresso and warm cream. Let the machine continue to run until the chocolate melts, until the mixture appears homogeneous.

Divide the mixture between two petite serving glasses.

Cover and chill in the fridge for at least 6 hours.

Serve with whipped cream and blood orange slices, if desired.

CHOCOLATE GANACHE CUPCAKES WITH PEPPERMINT CRUNCH
(or Sprinkles!)

A small batch of chocolate cupcakes with simple, perfect chocolate ganache. For the holidays, I love to top them with crushed candy canes. But every other month of the year, sprinkles work quite nicely.

Yield • 10 one-bite cupcakes

FOR THE CUPCAKES

⅓ cup all-purpose flour

2 tablespoons unsweetened cocoa powder

¼ teaspoon baking soda

¼ teaspoon baking powder

¼ teaspoon instant espresso powder (optional)

4 teaspoons canola oil

½ teaspoon vanilla extract

¼ cup lightly packed light brown sugar

⅓ cup low-fat buttermilk

TO MAKE THE CUPCAKES: Preheat the oven to 350°F, and line ten cups of a mini muffin pan with mini cupcake liners.

In a medium-size bowl, whisk together the flour, cocoa powder, baking soda, baking powder, and espresso powder, if using. Whisk well.

In a separate small bowl, whisk together the canola oil, vanilla, brown sugar, and buttermilk until well combined.

Pour the wet ingredients into the dry ingredients, and stir to combine. Do not overmix.

Bake the cupcakes for 8 to 11 minutes. Test a cupcake with a toothpick before removing from the oven. If moist crumbs cling to it, they're baked thoroughly.

Let the cupcakes cool in the pan for 1 minute, then transfer them to a wire rack to cool completely.

FOR THE CHOCOLATE GANACHE:

¼ cup dark chocolate chips

2 tablespoons unsalted butter

⅛ teaspoon peppermint extract
(or vanilla, if you're topping the
cupcakes with sprinkles)

2 crushed candy canes
(or sprinkles or nuts)

TO MAKE THE FROSTING: In a small bowl, melt the chocolate chips and butter in the microwave in 15-second intervals, stirring between each. It should only take 2–3 pulses. Stir in the peppermint or vanilla extract once the mixture is melted smooth.

Have the crushed candy canes or sprinkles ready in a shallow bowl. Dip the top of each cupcake in the melted chocolate, and then roll in the crushed candy canes or sprinkles.

You can let the chocolate harden in the fridge for 30 minutes, but do not store the cupcakes in the fridge any longer than that because the candy canes will soften.

YELLOW CAKE and CHOCOLATE FUDGE FROSTING

I've never been the type of girl to wait for a special occasion to open a bottle of champagne — Tuesday is a good enough reason for me. So, why not make this celebration cake any day of the year, too? Your favorite yellow, fluffy birthday cake with the richest chocolate fudge frosting is perfect for celebrating anything and absolutely nothing at the same time.

Yield • 1 (6-inch) cake

FOR THE CAKE
Cooking spray

1 large egg, separated

6 tablespoons unsalted butter, at room temperature

½ cup granulated sugar

¼ teaspoon vanilla extract

¾ cup all-purpose flour

⅛ teaspoon salt

¼ teaspoon baking soda

⅛ teaspoon baking powder

¼ cup buttermilk

Preheat the oven to 350°F. Spray a 6-inch round cake pan with cooking spray, and line the bottom of the pan with parchment paper.

TO MAKE THE CAKE: In a small bowl, using an electric mixer on high speed, beat the egg white until stiff peaks form.

In a separate bowl, using an electric mixer on medium speed, beat together the butter and granulated sugar until creamy, 1 to 2 minutes. Add the egg yolk and vanilla, and beat until combined.

In a third smaller bowl, whisk together the flour, salt, baking soda, and baking powder. Add half of the dry ingredients to the butter mixture and beat until combined. Add half of the buttermilk and beat. Add the remaining dry ingredients, stopping to beat until combined, and then finish with the last of the buttermilk. Gently fold the beaten egg white into the batter.

Scrape the batter into the prepared pan, and bake on a small baking sheet for 32 to 34 minutes, or until a toothpick inserted in the center comes out with only moist crumbs clinging to it. The cake will start to pull away from the edges when it's done, too. Don't underbake, or the cake will sink.

Let the cake cool completely.

FOR THE FROSTING
6 ounces semisweet chocolate chips

½ cup (1 stick, 4 ounces) butter, at room temperature

½ cup powdered sugar

⅓ cup unsweetened cocoa powder

½ teaspoon vanilla extract

Sprinkles (optional)

TO MAKE THE FROSTING: Melt the chocolate chips in a small dish in the microwave on low in 30-second pulses until melted. Stir between each pulse until the chocolate is smooth.

In a medium-size bowl, with an electric mixer on high speed, cream together the butter, powdered sugar, cocoa, and vanilla. Streak in the melted chocolate, and beat until fluffy.

Frost the cake, decorate with sprinkles, and serve.

In the first few years of our marriage, my husband and I moved three times. We did a little stint outside of Kansas City for about eighteen months, and we spent those months eating all of the barbecue in that great city. Kansas City knows its barbecue. And that means a lot, coming from this Texas girl. We chose new barbecue joints to visit a few times a month, all the while eating at Joe's Kansas City Barbecue as often as we could. We've still never found better ribs than Joe's Kansas City Barbecue, though we have tried.

One of the barbecue joints had very forgettable barbecue, but a completely unforgettable warm carrot cake for dessert. My husband, a carrot cake fiend (we even had a carrot wedding cake), ordered it off the menu. We were both surprised when it was served warm at the table with a melted cream cheese sauce for topping. We crave this version almost as much as the original version.

WARM CARROT CAKES WITH CREAM CHEESE SAUCE

Yield • 2 individual cakes

FOR THE CAKE
Cooking spray

2 tablespoons canola oil

5 tablespoons granulated sugar

1 large egg

½ teaspoon vanilla extract

¼ cup freshly grated carrot

6 tablespoons all-purpose flour

½ teaspoon ground cinnamon

¼ teaspoon ground ginger

⅛ teaspoon freshly grated nutmeg

⅛ teaspoon salt

FOR THE SAUCE
3 ounces cream cheese

1 tablespoons unsalted butter

5 tablespoons powdered sugar

¼ teaspoon vanilla extract

Preheat the oven to 350°F, and spray two 6-ounce ramekins very well with cooking spray. Place the ramekins on a small baking sheet.

TO MAKE THE CAKE: In a medium-size bowl, whisk together the oil, granulated sugar, egg, vanilla, and grated carrot.

Whisk together the remaining dry ingredients in a small bowl, and add to the wet ingredients. Stir until well combined.

Divide the mixture equally between the two prepared ramekins; the batter should come almost up to the inner line. Bake on the baking sheet for 23 to 25 minutes, until nicely domed and a toothpick inserted comes out with only moist crumbs.

TO MAKE THE SAUCE: In a small bowl, combine all the sauce ingredients, except the vanilla, and microwave on high in 30-second pulses until melted. Whisk together, and stir in the vanilla. Pour over the cakes and serve.

I loved anything my grandmother made, but these cookies have to be my all-time favorite. I literally cannot stop eating them. They're the perfect mixture of soft, chewy, and spicy. My grandma always used shortening in her cookies to give them that characteristic chew.

I scaled down her recipe to make just a dozen cookies, or else I would eat all five dozen by myself!

SOFT AND CHEWY GINGERSNAPS

Yield • 1 dozen cookies

¼ cup + 2 tablespoons vegetable shortening

½ cup granulated sugar, plus more for rolling

1 large egg white

2 tablespoons molasses (not blackstrap)

1 cup all-purpose flour

½ teaspoon ground ginger

½ teaspoon ground cinnamon

1 teaspoon baking soda

Preheat the oven to 350°F.

In a medium-size bowl, beat together the shortening and sugar until light and fluffy, about 2 minutes. Add the egg white and molasses and mix well. Add the remaining dry ingredients on top and beat until just combined.

Have ready a shallow bowl filled with extra sugar, for rolling the cookies.

Roll tablespoon-size chunks of dough into 1-inch balls. You should get about a dozen cookies. Roll each cookie in sugar. Bake on an ungreased cookie sheet for about 12 minutes.

Let cool on the baking sheet for 2 minutes before transferring them to a wire rack to cool completely. The cookies will be very soft, but they will firm up as they cool.

DOUBLE CHOCOLATE CHIP COOKIES

Sometimes, a chocolate chip cookie isn't enough. You need even more chocolate. Actually, *I* need even more chocolate. These chocolate cookies are studded with big chocolate chunks and sprinkled with salt before serving. They're every bit as dreamy as they sound.

Yield • 9 or 10 cookies

4 tablespoons unsalted butter, at room temperature

¼ cup + 2 tablespoons packed light brown sugar

1 large egg yolk

½ teaspoon vanilla extract

3 tablespoons unsweetened cocoa powder

½ cup all-purpose flour

¼ teaspoon instant espresso powder

¼ teaspoon baking soda

¼ teaspoon salt

¼ cup (heaping) chocolate chunks

Cooking spray (optional)

A pinch of large-grained salt, for sprinkling (optional)

In a medium-size bowl, beat the butter with an electric mixer on high speed until fluffy, about 1 minute. Add the brown sugar and beat for another minute. Add the egg yolk and vanilla and beat until well combined.

In a separate bowl, whisk together the cocoa powder, flour, espresso powder, baking soda, and salt until no lumps remain.

Add the dry ingredients to the wet ingredients in two increments, mixing between each addition. Finally, stir in the chocolate chunks.

Cover the dough and chill it for at least 1 hour. The dough can be made in advance or even frozen.

When ready to bake, preheat the oven to 350°F. Spray a cookie sheet with cooking spray or line it with parchment paper.

Scoop out nine or ten equal-size portions of dough and roll each in your hands to form a ball. Place each cookie at least 1 inch apart on the prepared cookie sheet.

Bake for 8 to 10 minutes. Check the cookies at 8 minutes—if they smell fragrant and the edges are set, remove them from the oven. Sprinkle with the salt, if using.

Let the cookies cool for 5 minutes on the baking sheet before serving.

1 DOZEN RUMMY OATMEAL COOKIES

I purposefully did not include the word *raisin* in the recipe title, because I know a lot of folks have serious disdain for raisins. I'm not sure why this is; they're just dried grapes. However, I think if you're a raisin hater, you just might be convinced with this recipe because I soak them in rum before stirring them into the cookie batter. If not, substitute chocolate chips.

Yield • 1 dozen cookies

½ cup raisins

2 tablespoons dark rum

3 tablespoons unsalted butter,
at room temperature

3 tablespoons light brown sugar

3 tablespoons granulated sugar

1 large egg yolk

¼ cup + 2 tablespoons all-purpose flour

¼ + ⅛ teaspoon baking powder

¼ teaspoon baking soda

¼ + ⅛ teaspoon ground cinnamon

⅛ teaspoon ground allspice

⅛ teaspoon salt

½ cup rolled oats

Preheat the oven to 350°F, and have ready a baking sheet.

In a small bowl, stir together the raisins and rum. Set aside and let soak.

In a medium-size bowl, cream together the butter and sugars for 1 to 2 minutes. Once thoroughly combined, add the egg yolk.

In a small bowl, whisk together the flour, baking powder, baking soda, cinnamon, allspice, and salt. Add half of the flour mixture to the butter mixture, mixing until just combined. Add the remaining flour mixture, and beat until combined. Do not overmix. Stir in the oats and raisins (include any rum that was not absorbed).

Divide equally into twelve balls, and space 1 inch apart on the baking sheet.

Bake for 13 to 15 minutes, or until golden brown. Don't be afraid to let these cookies get a little color — the browned butter and rum flavor combo is delicious.

MINI BREAD PUDDINGS . . .
with brown sugar whiskey caramel

I'm a newly converted bread pudding fan. I'm not sure what took me so long. Maybe it's because I never had bread pudding with a brown sugar whiskey caramel sauce until I made it for you. Allllllllll for you.

Yield • 6 mini bread puddings

3 tablespoons unsalted butter, divided

¼ cup pecan halves

Oil or cooking spray, for pan

½ cup milk

½ cup heavy whipping cream

¼ cup granulated sugar

½ teaspoon ground cinnamon

Pinch of freshly grated nutmeg

½ teaspoon vanilla extract

¼ teaspoon almond extract

1 large egg + 1 large egg yolk

2 ½ cups white bread cubes (from about 3 slices of bread)

Place 1 tablespoon of the butter in a small skillet and turn the heat to medium-low. Add the pecans when the butter melts, and toast gently until fragrant and beginning to darken in several places. Remove from the heat and pour into a bowl immediately, to stop the cooking process.

Preheat the oven to 325°F, and grease six cups of a muffin pan with oil or cooking spray.

Melt the remaining 2 tablespoons of butter in a medium-size bowl. Whisk in the milk, cream, granulated sugar, cinnamon, nutmeg, vanilla, and almond extract. Don't be tempted to skip the almond extract; it's pivotal here. If you're out, though, use an extra bump of vanilla in its place. Finally, stir in the egg and egg yolk.

Add the bread cubes, stir, and let sit for 5 minutes.

Divide the bread cube mixture equally among the prepared muffin cups, not worrying so much about the liquid. After all of the bread is divided, even out the amount of liquid between the cups—it should fill about three fourths of the way in each cup.

Bake the bread puddings for 20 minutes.

After 20 minutes, scatter the pecans and any excess butter on top, and return the bread puddings to the oven for another 7 to 10 minutes.

Let the puddings cool in the pan for 10 minutes before removing with a knife.

FOR THE BROWN SUGAR WHISKEY CARAMEL SAUCE

¼ cup dark brown sugar

3 tablespoons heavy whipping cream

Splash of whiskey

TO MAKE THE SAUCE: Place the brown sugar and cream in a small saucepan or butter warmer. Bring to a boil and cook for 2 minutes. Remove from the heat, and stir in the whiskey.

Drizzle the sauce over the cooled bread puddings and serve.

STRAWBERRY SKILLET COBBLER

Think of this as strawberry shortcake, made all in one pan. Just add whipped cream on top before serving. Or serve it right out of the oven with ice cream, like a cobbler. No matter how you serve it, this springtime dessert will be your favorite way to enjoy strawberries. If berries aren't in season, no problem; just use frozen berries.

The 8-inch skillet that I use for this cobbler for two is most likely the smallest skillet that came in your pots and pans set. I think it's meant for scrambled eggs, but let's use it for dessert for two, okay?

Yield • 1 (8-inch) cobbler

1 pound frozen strawberries

2 tablespoons granulated sugar, plus more for sprinkling

Zest and juice of 1 small lemon

2 tablespoons cornstarch

Freshly grated nutmeg, for sprinkling

FOR THE BISCUIT DOUGH
¾ cup all-purpose flour

¾ teaspoon baking powder

¼ teaspoon baking soda

Pinch of salt

3 tablespoons cold unsalted butter

¼ cup milk

Preheat the oven to 400°F.

Pour the frozen strawberries in an 8-inch skillet. Add the sugar, lemon zest, and lemon juice, and place over medium-low heat. Bring to a simmer just to release some of the juices and slightly defrost the berries. Do not overcook. Remove from the heat, and stir in the cornstarch.

TO MAKE THE BISCUIT DOUGH: Combine the flour, baking powder, baking soda, and salt in a small bowl. Dice the butter, and add it to the bowl. Use your fingertips or a pastry blender to blend the butter into the flour mixture. The butter should be evenly distributed and smaller than peas. Add the milk, and stir until a shaggy dough forms.

Dollop the dough in five large clumps over the berries, then sprinkle with sugar and nutmeg. Bake for 18 to 20 minutes, until the berries are bubbling and the biscuits have browned.

A SMALL BATCH OF HOMEMADE MARSHMALLOWS

I dreamed of making homemade marshmallows for a long time before I actually tackled the recipe. I assumed homemade marshmallows would be time-consuming and difficult. It couldn't be further from the truth. I can get these marshmallows in the pan in 20 minutes. They take 3 hours to set into the perfect marshmallow consistency, but that's not bad for only 20 minutes of work.

Be sure to "flour" your surface generously with powdered sugar, and use parchment paper. Once, I made this recipe using waxed paper and was disappointed when the 'mallows stuck to the paper. Parchment paper is the only nonstick surface you can use here.

This recipe makes eight big marshmallows. Use them to top sweet potatoes (page 118), or plop them in steaming mugs of hot chocolate (page 205).

Yield • 8 large marshmallows

¾ cup granulated sugar

⅓ cup light corn syrup

Pinch of salt

6 tablespoons cool water

1 packet (2 ½ teaspoons) unflavored gelatin powder

½ vanilla bean, or ½ teaspoon vanilla extract

Cooking spray, unsalted butter, or oil, for pan

¾ cup powdered sugar

In a medium-size saucepan, stir together the granulated sugar, corn syrup, salt, and 3 tablespoons of the water. Turn the heat to high and bring to a boil without stirring. Clip a candy thermometer to the edge of the pan, and boil until the mixture reaches 238°F.

Meanwhile, place the remaining 3 tablespoons of water in a large bowl and sprinkle the gelatin evenly on top. Let sit for a few minutes without stirring.

When the sugar syrup reaches 238°F, slowly begin to stream it into the gelatin mixture while beating constantly with a hand mixer (not a stand mixer) on medium speed. Do not splash the syrup on the edges of the bowl, or it will harden immediately. Go slow, and take your time. Beat the mixture for a full 10 minutes.

Stir in the vanilla bean seeds or vanilla until combined.

Spread the mixture into a 9 × 5 × 3-inch loaf pan that has been lined with parchment paper and greased very well with cooking spray, butter, or oil.

Let the mixture set, uncovered, for at least 3 hours.

When ready to cut, sprinkle the powdered sugar on a work surface. Dump out the marshmallows onto the sugared surface and slice, dipping the knife in powdered sugar between cuts.

Store the marshmallows in an airtight container at room temperature. They will keep for 2 to 3 days.

TWO MUGS OF HOT CHOCOLATE

Just in case you need something to float all those pretty homemade marshmallows in . . .

Yield • 2 mugs

2 tablespoons semisweet chocolate chips

4 tablespoons unsweetened cocoa powder

2 tablespoons powdered sugar

2 cups milk

Marshmallows (page 202), for garnish

For each mug, place 1 tablespoon of chocolate chips in the bottom. Top with 2 tablespoons of the cocoa powder and 1 tablespoon of the powdered sugar. Repeat for the second mug.

Heat the milk in the microwave on high until steamy and small bubbles form around the edges. Once the milk is hot, slowly stream it in the mugs while whisking constantly. The milk should melt the chocolate chips, but if the milk isn't hot enough, cover the mugs with a plate for 60 seconds, then whisk again.

Enjoy with marshmallows on top!

TWO MUGS OF EGGNOG

The thing about eggnog is that it's usually made in large punchbowl quantities. This is great for parties, but what if it's chilly outside and you just want a couple mugs of it? I have you covered. This recipe is scaled down perfectly for two, plus it doesn't contain any pesky uncooked eggs, so you can serve it to anyone. The traditional version includes beaten egg whites, so I give you that option, too. I think it tastes like melted ice cream, and I've been known to drink it chilled in the summer!

Yield · 2 mugs

2 large eggs, separated

3 tablespoons granulated sugar

1 cup whole milk

½ to ¾ cup heavy whipping cream (see tip below)

¾ teaspoon freshly grated nutmeg, divided

2 shots bourbon whiskey

In a medium-size bowl, whisk the egg yolks with the sugar until pale yellow and tripled in size. I do this by hand with a big balloon whisk, and it takes about 1 minute. Whisk vigorously.

Meanwhile, in a 1-quart saucepan, heat the milk, ½ cup of the cream, and ½ teaspoon of the freshly grated nutmeg to boiling. Remove from the heat.

While whisking continuously, very slowly stream the milk mixture into the egg yolks. Go slowly to avoid scrambling the eggs.

Pour the entire mixture back into the saucepan, and place over medium heat. Stirring occasionally, heat the mixture to 160°F.

OPTIONAL: If you want to be traditional and fold egg whites into your eggnog, go ahead and whip the two remaining egg whites to stiff peaks. When the eggnog reaches 160°F, remove it from the heat and gently fold in the beaten egg whites.

Chill the mixture thoroughly if you want to serve it cold. Before serving, divide it between two mugs, add bourbon to taste, and sprinkle with the remaining ¼ teaspoon of nutmeg.

TIP *If folding the leftover egg whites into the mixture, use ½ cup of cream. If not, use ¾ cup of cream.*

Acknowledgments

It's a good thing in life to owe so many people thank yous and I love yous. I may be at an all-time high with this book.

I want to share a special thanks to QVC for seeing something in me, and pushing to make this book happen. I'm so grateful to you. A very warm, heartfelt thanks goes to David Venable. Oh, David, when you walk into a room, it fills with light, and I'm so happy to be next to you in that light.

Thanks to the Norton team for helping me pull this book together. It wasn't easy, and the deadlines were tight, but somehow, we beat the clock before I went into labor! That reminds me—thanks for putting up with my hormonal swings during pregnancy.

To my agent and friend, Jean Sagendorph. I love it when you call me with good news. Most of all, I love taking on the world with you.

And last but not least, to my readers. To you empty nesters, couples, singles, young and old. Every time you write me to say my recipes fulfill your craving without extra leftovers, I am reminded why I do this. (I do this so we don't eat an entire cake in one sitting, right?)

All my love,
Christina

Index